# Winning isn't Everything

Stories, Poems, Essays, Sermons

*Gerald M. Siegel*

*To Harold and Ella, Dear Friends!*

*Jerry*

Morton Publishing
Edina, Minnesota

Copyright © 2013 by Gerald M. Siegel

All rights reserved. No material in this book may be copied or reproduced in any form or by any electronic or mechanical means, including information storage-and-retrieval systems, without the express written consent of the author, except for brief quotations in critical articles and reviews.

Printed in the United States of America

The following stories were previously published, though in different form: "Stonis Orchidus: Parable of the Rock" appeared in *The Star Tribune* and the *Brooklyn College Review*; "Family Conspiracy," "He Might Have Been Champ," "The King's Adviser," "Where Are Joshua's Glasses?" (also in *Opti-Courier*), "The Most Famous Man in the World," "New Year's Prayer" all appeared in *Identity*; "Shtey Glaykh" in *Voices of Conservative Judaism* and *Der Bay*; "There's Bears in There" in the *Cook County Star*; "A New Silk Coat" and "Laundry Day" in *Western Cleaners and Launderers*; "Visiting Day" and "Richard Dyer-Bennet" in *Green's Magazine*. The following stories appeared in *Handball Magazine*: "Handball Fantasy" (also in the Star-Tribune), "Minutes of the Meeting," "The Cooke Hall Consortium," "He Might Have Been Champ," "The Spirit Endureth," "Winning Isn't Everything," and "Handball Hype." "Teacher's Roll: Scenes from a Lectern" appeared in *Minnesota Monthly*; "The Lost Chord" in *Music Teacher* magazine; "Elijah's Cup" and "The Four Questions" in *American Jewish World*.

Cover design by Cathy Spengler
Book design by Corey Sevett

ISBN: 978-1492140030

Published in the United States by

MORTON PUBLISHING
5501 VILLAGE DRIVE 105
EDINA, MN 55439

For my grandchildren,
Jacob, Elana, Allison, and Zachary,
who made this book necessary;
and Eileen, who made it possible.

ALSO BY GERALD M. SIEGEL

*You Shoulda Been There*

# Contents

Preface .................................................................. ix

## STORIES

Stonis Orchidus: Parable of the Rock............................... 1
The Ant and the Grasshopper: Aesop's Fable, Freely Adapted ......... 3
Family Conspiracy .................................................. 5
*Shtey Glaykh:* A Lesson in Yiddish ................................ 11
Happy Birthday, Mom ............................................... 17
There's Bears in There ............................................ 25
Where Are Joshua's Glasses? ....................................... 29
Piano Bentsh ...................................................... 35
A Ring for Every Finger ........................................... 39
A New Silk Coat ................................................... 45
Laundry Day ....................................................... 49
Visiting Day ...................................................... 53
Driving Lessons ................................................... 57
Teacher's Roll: Scenes from a Lectern ............................. 61
Two Out in the Bottom of the Ninth ................................ 69
Turtle Mania ...................................................... 73
The Quality of Mercy .............................................. 77
Richard Dyer-Bennet ............................................... 81
A Grand Idea ...................................................... 87

## HANDBALL STORIES

Handball Fantasy .................................................. 91
Minutes of the Meeting ............................................ 93
The Cooke Hall Consortium ......................................... 97
He Might Have Been Champ ......................................... 101
The Spirit Endureth .............................................. 107
Winning Isn't Everything ......................................... 111
Handball Hype .................................................... 115

## FROM THE PULPIT

Akedah (Genesis 22:1—24) ......................................... 121
Vayishlach (Genesis 32:4—36:43) .................................. 125
Beha'alotecha (Numbers, 8:1—12:16) ............................... 129

Shlach L'cha-1 (Numbers, 13:1—15:41) . . . . . . . . . . . . . . . . . . . . . . . 133
Shlach L'cha-2 (Numbers, 13:1—15:41) . . . . . . . . . . . . . . . . . . . . . . . 139
Korah (Numbers 16:1 —18:32) . . . . . . . . . . . . . . . . . . . . . . . . . . . . . . 143
Balak (Numbers 22:2—25:9) . . . . . . . . . . . . . . . . . . . . . . . . . . . . . . . . 149
Va'etchanan (Deuteronomy 3:23—7:11) . . . . . . . . . . . . . . . . . . . . . . . 155
Ekev (Deuteronomy 7:12—11:22) . . . . . . . . . . . . . . . . . . . . . . . . . . . 161
Ki Tetze (Deuteronomy 21:10—25:19) . . . . . . . . . . . . . . . . . . . . . . . . 163
Re'eh (Deuteronomy 11:26 —16:17) . . . . . . . . . . . . . . . . . . . . . . . . . 167
Ki Tavo (Deuteronomy 26:1—29:8) . . . . . . . . . . . . . . . . . . . . . . . . . . 171
Nitzavim (Deuteronomy 29:9—30:20) . . . . . . . . . . . . . . . . . . . . . . . 175

## THE CHILDREN'S CORNER
The Most Famous Man in the World . . . . . . . . . . . . . . . . . . . . . . . . . 181
The King's Adviser . . . . . . . . . . . . . . . . . . . . . . . . . . . . . . . . . . . . . . . 185
Dror and Parrot's Bar Mitzvah . . . . . . . . . . . . . . . . . . . . . . . . . . . . . . 191
The Day the Ark Almost Sank . . . . . . . . . . . . . . . . . . . . . . . . . . . . . . 195
The Four Questions . . . . . . . . . . . . . . . . . . . . . . . . . . . . . . . . . . . . . . 201
Jacob's Flying Birthday Party . . . . . . . . . . . . . . . . . . . . . . . . . . . . . . . 203
Birthday Radio Broadcast . . . . . . . . . . . . . . . . . . . . . . . . . . . . . . . . . 207
It's a Math, Math World . . . . . . . . . . . . . . . . . . . . . . . . . . . . . . . . . . 209
The Lost Chord . . . . . . . . . . . . . . . . . . . . . . . . . . . . . . . . . . . . . . . . . 211
To Be or Not to Be—Seven Years Old . . . . . . . . . . . . . . . . . . . . . . . . 215
The Adventures of Elana Siegel . . . . . . . . . . . . . . . . . . . . . . . . . . . . . 217
Allison's Birthday Party . . . . . . . . . . . . . . . . . . . . . . . . . . . . . . . . . . . 221
Elijah's Cup . . . . . . . . . . . . . . . . . . . . . . . . . . . . . . . . . . . . . . . . . . . . 225
A Tree for Rosh Hashanah . . . . . . . . . . . . . . . . . . . . . . . . . . . . . . . . . 227
Zachary Goes for a Ride . . . . . . . . . . . . . . . . . . . . . . . . . . . . . . . . . . 231

## ASSORTED POEMS WITH CHILDREN IN MIND
Colic . . . . . . . . . . . . . . . . . . . . . . . . . . . . . . . . . . . . . . . . . . . . . . . . . . 234
Rain . . . . . . . . . . . . . . . . . . . . . . . . . . . . . . . . . . . . . . . . . . . . . . . . . . 235
Koala . . . . . . . . . . . . . . . . . . . . . . . . . . . . . . . . . . . . . . . . . . . . . . . . . 236
Giraffe . . . . . . . . . . . . . . . . . . . . . . . . . . . . . . . . . . . . . . . . . . . . . . . . 238
The Shrinking Giraffe . . . . . . . . . . . . . . . . . . . . . . . . . . . . . . . . . . . . 239
Cats . . . . . . . . . . . . . . . . . . . . . . . . . . . . . . . . . . . . . . . . . . . . . . . . . . 240
Last Night I Saw the Moon . . . . . . . . . . . . . . . . . . . . . . . . . . . . . . . . 241
Now You Are Two . . . . . . . . . . . . . . . . . . . . . . . . . . . . . . . . . . . . . . . 242
Zachary at Five . . . . . . . . . . . . . . . . . . . . . . . . . . . . . . . . . . . . . . . . . 243
Elana Is Six . . . . . . . . . . . . . . . . . . . . . . . . . . . . . . . . . . . . . . . . . . . . 244
I Planted Some Flowers . . . . . . . . . . . . . . . . . . . . . . . . . . . . . . . . . . . 246
Tradition . . . . . . . . . . . . . . . . . . . . . . . . . . . . . . . . . . . . . . . . . . . . . . 248

    Purim Poem. . . . . . . . . . . . . . . . . . . . . . . . . . . . . . . . . . . . . . . . . . . . . . 251
    Twelve Verses for a Twelve-Year-Old. . . . . . . . . . . . . . . . . . . . . . . . . . . 252

**LETTERS FROM THE MINNESOTA TOOTH FAIRY** . . . . . . . . . . . . . . . . 255

**IN CONCLUSION**
    To Forgive Is Divine . . . . . . . . . . . . . . . . . . . . . . . . . . . . . . . . . . . . . . . . 266
    New Year's Prayer . . . . . . . . . . . . . . . . . . . . . . . . . . . . . . . . . . . . . . . . . 267

# Preface

In 2012 I self-published fifty-three stories and essays in a book I called *You Shoulda Been There*. That collection traced my experiences growing up in a mixed Jewish-Italian neighborhood in Brooklyn, moving to Iowa for graduate education, experiencing the Midwest for the first time, and ending up in Minnesota, where I settled with family and became integrated into a Jewish community very different from the one I knew as a youth. Included too were stories of my sojourn in North Dakota and Kansas, a sabbatical in Israel, holiday celebrations, and stories that were pure fiction.

The current book, *Winning Isn't Everything*, is more eclectic; it includes miscellaneous stories, heroic tales from the handball court, children's stories and poems, and correspondence with the Minnesota tooth fairy. The target for some of this collection was originally family, but I hope it will appeal to a wider audience. After all, who hasn't been in intimate communication with the tooth fairy, or a child with colic, or a refrigerator that goes "clunk" and then becomes ominously silent? I have also included a selection of sermons I have given over the years at my synagogue, Adath Jeshurun, at the invitation of the rabbi.

Some of the stories in this collection have been previously published. All have been revised and edited for the current book.

John Toren edited all of written material in the book, and provided other valuable services to bring the project to fruition. The covers were designed by Cathy Spengler. The photo on the front cover was taken by Eileen Siegel, and shows the author and grandson Zachary Jacobs in fierce combat. On the back cover, Siegel is entertaining a group assembled to celebrate Richard McDermott's 83$^{1}/_{3}$rd birthday at the Doubletree Hotel in St. Louis Park, Minnesota. Corey Sevett designed the interior of the book and was very forgiving of the author's foibles. Ilze Mueller was copy editor. All were generous with their time and talent.

Publication of this book was supported by a grant from the Office of the Vice President for Research and the University of Minnesota Retirees Association (UMRA).

Gerald M. Siegel
Edina, Minnesota
2013

# Stories

# Stonis Orchidus: Parable of the Rock

ONCE, IN A FAR-OFF LAND, there was a magical garden filled with lovely flowers that bloomed throughout the year, without regard to the seasons. Off in one corner of this garden sat a rock. By comparison with the luxuriant flowers, it was dull and plain, undistinguished in form, color, or fragrance.

One day a delicate orchid growing nearby leaned toward the rock and spoke.

"Pardon me, sir, but what sort of creature are you and why are you in this garden? You offer no delights to the eyes or nose. You are utterly devoid of charm or beauty."

The rock hesitated for a moment and then answered, "Madam, I am your cousin. I too am an orchid."

The orchid recoiled and arched its neck. "You? An orchid?! How presumptuous! You're nothing but a shapeless clod, a lump."

"So it may seem," intoned the rock, "but I am in truth an extraordinary orchid, fashioned in the shape of a rock. I am of the rare botanical variety *Stonis Orchidus*."

The orchid laughed. "What an absurd conceit. You an orchid! You are nothing but…"

At that moment the orchid's speech was abruptly terminated by a gardener's shears as he cut its stem and handed the flower to the mistress of the garden. She smiled and held the delicate flower to her fickle bosom, until, a short while later, her attention was captured by other pleasures and the orchid was cast aside.

Each day the mistress walked in her garden, taking a fancy to one or another of the flowers, which were then dutifully offered up to her by the gardener. The rock observed all and stonily remained in its place, pleasing none, but enduring, enduring.

One afternoon, just after the gardener had charmed his lady by beheading an iris, the rock sighed softly, thereby catching the attention of a yellow rose. The rose inclined slightly in the direction of the rock and spoke haughtily, "I can't imagine why you're here, unless it's to mark a contrast with the rest of us. You're certainly ugly enough."

The rock gazed at the rose, noting its alluring color and noble bearing. "Madam, I am your cousin, an extraordinary rose shaped like a rock, grown in Estonia. I am *Tabla Rosa*."

The yellow rose shook with laughter. "Tabla Rosa indeed. A rock by any other name is still a rock, you arrogant lump."

Before the rock could respond, the gardener, attracted perhaps by the graceful movement in the flower bed, thought to win his mistress' approval by bringing her, unbidden, a colorful bouquet. The yellow rose was prominent in its midst.

There were other such encounters with the treasures of the garden, and over the years the rock revealed itself to be a great variety of exotic flowers: Clump Ivy, Petrified Peony, Calcified Carnation, while always remaining, immutably, a rock.

Then one day, a transformation took place deep in the core of the rock. On that day, a tulip scornfully addressed the rock in tones that had become quite familiar. "I can't imagine why so unappealing a creature as you is allowed in our garden. What exactly are you?"

For a moment the rock was silent. It gazed at the tulip's delicate petals and intoxicating color. A bead of dew glistened on the flower, a further crown to its beauty. Deep within the rock was a voice that wanted to cry out: "I too was fashioned out of love by our Creator; I too have a place in His universe; I too am beautiful and desirable."

This voice was stilled. What was heard instead was the voice of eons of enduring, of constancy, and finally, pride.

"Madam, I am a rock."

# The Ant and the Grasshopper: Aesop's Fable, Freely Adapted

ALL SUMMER ANT diligently gathered food and set it aside for the long, harsh winter. She never paused to smell a rose or to lie in the sun. She worked, and worked, and worked. For her the summer was as dark as winter because she spent most of it storing provisions in tunnels below the ground.

During this same summer, Grasshopper romped in the sun, kicked up her heels, smelled all the roses she could find, and cheerfully serenaded her busy friend.

When winter came, the ground froze and was covered with snow, and food was scarce. Grasshopper began to feel pangs of hunger. It occurred to her to visit Ant. She entered her friend's anteroom anticipating a warm welcome.

Instead, Ant said peevishly, "My dear Hopper, how can you possibly be out of food already? What happened to the stores you set aside for winter?"

"But I have no stores, dear Antie," said Grasshopper. "I only have songs and sonnets and a bit of haiku."

"What did you do all summer, then, while I was laboring?" asked Ant.

"Oh," said Grasshopper, recalling the summer with a broad smile, "I played and frolicked and sang songs to make your labors go easier. Shall I sing you a song now?"

Ant interrupted before Grasshopper could trill the first delicate notes. "You sang, you lazy and frivolous insect? Very well. Now go out in the cold and dance!" With that, she pushed Grasshopper out and slammed the door.

For a moment Grasshopper was shocked. She was not accustomed to such rude treatment, especially from someone she considered a friend. But then she brightened.

"Why, the old dear is absolutely correct," she said to herself. "What good advice." Without further hesitation she raised herself up in the classic First Hopper Position and gracefully danced out of Ant's cold hallway and into the much warmer world of snow, ice, and wind.

She jumped and twirled until she forgot all about mean-spirited Ant. She danced up a sunset and a full moon and a sky resplendent with stars. She danced away her hunger and her cares. She danced and danced. And she sang, too, as the snow fell relentlessly, turning the whole earth into a glittering ballroom under the lights of the delighted moon and the applauding, twinkling stars.

# Family Conspiracy

AFTER TWENTY-TWO YEARS it seemed only right that Eileen and I should have a romantic fling, the two of us sneaking off for a night in a fancy hotel, savoring the novelty, the *sheer self-indulgence*. We'd never done anything like it, but now, finally, the time was right. My mother had been visiting us for ten days and was to fly home to New York on Sunday. On Monday the children returned to school, but the university was closed and I had a day off. Laurie, the children's favorite babysitter, would sleep at the house with them Sunday night and make sure they got off to school properly in the morning. Eileen and I would drive my mother to the airport and then, instead of returning home, we would commence our romantic tryst.

The plan was perfect except for one complication—my wife. I was certain she would never agree to anything so frivolous. There were a dozen items on our list, a dozen better ways to spend money. All reasonable, of course, but….No! For once I would not be ruled by reason. For once romantic exuberance would triumph over good sense. But it was clear I would need help to make the plan work; it would require no less than a family conspiracy.

One by one I recruited my fellow conspirators. Karen, our fourteen-year-old daughter, was given the most delicate assignment. She was to pick out the clothes Eileen would need and then pack them in a suitcase where Eileen wouldn't find it. Karen was ecstatic. This was precisely the kind of adventure her poetic nature thrived on. She could barely contain her excitement.

"Shh," I warned her. "All the preparations have to be done quietly and with stealth. Your mother mustn't have a clue, or all will be lost."

"Yes. Yes," Karen answered gleefully in a stage whisper that would fill an auditorium. "You just get me a suitcase and I'll have it packed."

"All right," I said, "but remember, no one must know of this but you and I and David. Not a word to Josh; he's sure to spill the beans. And don't tell Grandma, either. She might decide that Laurie is too young to stay with you and feel obliged to prolong her visit."

Later that afternoon I brought a suitcase already containing my clothes into Karen's room where it immediately became invisible among the clutter and disarray. Now the operation began in earnest. We needed to distract Eileen while Karen packed her clothing.

My second recruit, our fifteen-year-old son, David, provided a diversionary maneuver.

"Mom!" he called passionately from the head of the stairs. "A couple of buttons came off my Scout shirt. I can't go to Scouts tomorrow without my shirt."

He held the shirt for her to see, the freshly cut threads dangling conspicuously. Eileen peered at him strangely for a moment, then collected the shirt and retreated to the sewing room holding it at arm's length as though it might be infected with some odd virus.

Karen, meanwhile, had raced into our bedroom where she began pulling assorted garments from Eileen's dresser. Giggling with delight, she thrust them one after another into the suitcase. She had just returned to the living room with a beatific expression on her face when Eileen reappeared, the diseased shirt still thrust out in front of her, but with all the buttons once again in their proper places.

I gazed inquiringly at Karen. Done? She shook her head slightly. Not quite. There was need for a second foray, and that meant another diversion. Our eight-year-old son, Josh, inadvertently came to the rescue. There was a loud crash from the kitchen, followed by a loud "Oh, no!" We found Josh sprawled on the kitchen floor, covered with flour.

"I was just looking to see if there was any candy hidden in the cupboard, and the stool slipped, and I fell, and everything spilled."

In the flurry of sweeping and brushing and sneezing that followed, Karen's absence was not noticed. She disappeared to grab for combs, brushes, cosmetics, and a few more articles of clothing. Eileen, hearing an uncommon amount of drawers opening and closing, rushed to the bedroom to avoid yet another calamity. There was Karen, clutching a blouse and a skirt.

"Karen, what is going on here? Why are you holding my clothes? What is happening to everybody in this house today? Your grandmother will think we've all gone berserk just as she's leaving—or maybe 'escaping' would be a better term."

"Nothing, Mom. Really. We're going to have a '50s dance at school later in the spring. I was looking in your closet to see what might work."

"I'll have you know that none of my clothes are from the '50s. Or hardly any. And I certainly hope you weren't planning to wear that blouse with that skirt. Our taste was never that bad. Not even in the '50s."

Clever Karen. For the next fifteen minutes she was treated to a lecture on proper dress, complete with a demonstration of tasteless combinations, and topped off with a minor discourse on modesty. When, finally, they both appeared again, Karen could hardly suppress a triumphant grin. That evening I noticed that my two older children treated me with a new regard: Neat, cool, really rude, they whispered.

The children finally went to bed, as did my mother, who was already contemplating her return home. It was quiet. So quiet that I could hear doubts and misgivings begin to resonate in my mind: It will never work. Something will go wrong. Eileen will insist that it's a dumb idea, that we should turn around and go home. I'll be disappointed, but that will be nothing compared to the children's feelings. They'll be devastated. I couldn't let that happen. Finally I broke the silence. "Eileen, there's something I've been keeping from you…"

She looked up from her book and said, "Say no more. I forgive all. We must think of the children and not ourselves. …"

It was my turn to interrupt. "Wait a minute. This is me, not Dr. Zhivago."

A trace of disappointment crossed her face as I dragged her out of her reverie. I went on. "I've got something to tell you. I've planned a surprise. The kids are in on it. Tomorrow, after we take my mother to the airport, we're not coming straight home."

"Where are we going?"

"The plan is for Laurie to stay with the kids and for you and me to spend the night at the Sofitel. You're not supposed to have a clue."

"Then why are you telling me now?"

"Because I'm afraid you won't like the idea, that you'll remind me of all the practical things we could better spend our money on, and that I'll have to disappoint the kids."

"Shh," she said. "Don't go on so. It's a wonderful idea, and not because of the children."

"You mean it? You're really pleased?"

"Of course I am."

"What a relief! Then everything is set. Our clothes are packed. Karen picked out yours. They're in a suitcase in her room."

"Fine," Eileen said, "I'll just sneak in while she's sleeping and see what she chose."

"But quietly. We don't want the children to know I've got a new partner in deception and intrigue."

A new partner. What was needed now was a new conspiracy to protect the original conspiracy. The children were not to know that Eileen knew. We had raised the intrigue one level. Now we had agents and double agents.

The morning broke with a bustle of activity. The children were everywhere, attending to their grandmother, in our room, guarding the suitcase, lurking in the hallways, giggling and consorting together. Josh had finally been told the secret and a huge effort was expended keeping him from blurting it out. Eileen walked benignly through the turmoil, seeing and hearing all, while feigning to understand nothing. The children marveled at her obtuseness. She didn't notice them repeatedly huddling, their veiled looks and sudden laughter, the suitcase dragged out of the house and into the trunk of the car. Not a thing.

Eileen, warming to her part, took some ground beef from the freezer and pointedly remarked, "I'll make a meatloaf for dinner tonight, after we get back from dropping Grandma at the airport." The children snickered. "Are you sure you don't want to come with us?" Eileen asked innocently.

Josh started to assent but a hand was quickly placed over his mouth.

"No—I mean, I'd like to," David said, "but I've got to do some homework for tomorrow."

"Me too," Karen chimed in.

Eileen looked properly amazed at these atypical evidences of industry.

"Well, all right. But don't go running off someplace. I want you all home when we get back."

"But you aren't…." Josh started to offer, only to be interrupted by a candy jammed into his mouth. "Sure, Mom. Sure," they answered eagerly.

It was time to leave. "Goodbye, Grandma," the children called out. "Have a good trip. You too, Mom and Dad, have a good trip."

"But we aren't going anywhere…." Eileen's voice trailed off as the car pulled away. Through the mirror, I could see them waving exuberantly.

Not long afterward, I stood at the front desk of the Sofitel, just as I had imagined.

"Mr. and Mrs. Siegel," I announced to the clerk. "We have a reservation." As I spoke, I averted my eyes, suddenly feeling shy. I turned and saw that Eileen was already at the elevator, looking impatient.

"Hurry up," she beckoned. "I'm waiting for you."

# *Shtey Glaykh:*
# A Lesson in Yiddish

I COULD HAVE LEARNED Yiddish from my grandparents or from listening in on conversations among my neighbors, most of whom were immigrants from Eastern Europe, but in those days I wasn't at all interested. Now, at an advanced age, I have discovered the joys of Yiddish, but find my brain is no longer adept at taking it in, much less retaining any of it. Back then, on Sundays, it was my job to deliver bagels, onion rolls, bialys, and the Yiddish newspapers to my grandparents, who lived just a few blocks from us in Bensonhurst, Brooklyn. I also collected the *Daily Mirror* and the *Brooklyn Eagle* for Uncle Abe, who moved in with them after he came back from the Navy. Later in the day, the extended family would assemble at my grandparents' home for herring, boiled potatoes, tea served in *yahrzeit* glasses, loud discussion—and, for the battle tested, a spirited game of pinochle.

Not everyone would play. Uncle Abe would be on the town by then; my father didn't enjoy the rough-and-tumble of the game. Uncle Joe would be reading or dozing, waiting for Uncle Meyer so they could discuss the grocery business. Uncle Meyer and Ann-Meyer's would arrive, their Pontiac parked on the street, and also Seymour and Ann-Seymour's (I was an adult before I realized that "Ann-Seymour's" and "Ann-Meyer's" were not proper names). Later, Uncle Ben and Tante Chaika would come, scattering coins for the children and baked goods for the adults in unstated competition with my grandmother. Then some Yiddish might be spoken. I didn't pay attention. I was eating *mandl broyt* and counting my coins.

The kids, my generation, would be wandering around the small apartment. How did we all fit in? I recently heard of a young couple with one child who bought a huge house—six thousand square feet on one floor. I can't imagine living in all that space. How would they find each other to fight or argue? Too much space is like too much freedom, a plague rather than a blessing.

Later in the week, when it was just my grandfather and me, he again became a tailor rather than a cardsharp. "*Shtey glaykh!*" he would mutter through the pins in his mouth, down on his knees, as he made marks with his soap chalk and pinned the fabric that would become my trousers. I didn't know the words, but I knew that I had better be still or I would endure a pinprick or, worse yet, his exasperation. "*Shtey glaykh*" is the Yiddish expression I recall most vividly, because it was spoken by my grandfather and directed to me. I also knew from my grandmother that I was a "*bubele*," "*ziskayt*," "*miskayt*," "*kluge yung*," "*langer loksh*," and a "*khalerye*," and that all of those meant I was someone special.

While I was growing up, Yiddish newspapers sat alongside Italian papers on the newsstand at Izzie's candy store. Shops along Eighteenth Avenue had notices posted in Yiddish. I overheard it in the market, and on the subway and the trolley that ran along New Utrecht Avenue. On Passover I recited the "*Fir Kashes*" (Four Questions) in Yiddish to tumultuous applause. The applause was only partly for my performance. At our highly abbreviated seder the recitation of the Four Questions also meant that the chicken soup would soon be on the table. The rabbi at our small Orthodox synagogue gave sermons during the High Holy Days in Yiddish and I have a faint recollection of giving my memorized Bar Mitzvah speech in Yiddish, though I understood nothing that I was saying.

Italian was also ubiquitous in our mixed neighborhood. I loved the sound of Italian much more than Yiddish. Italian was a "Romance language" and I yearned for romance. Yiddish was the *Mama Loshn* (mother tongue) at a time when I was trying to break away from Mama; it was the *loshn* of the ancient rabbi in my synagogue, of places left behind, destroyed, abandoned. I chose not to learn Yiddish. Or at least I thought I did.

In 1954, married for a year, I left Brooklyn to do doctoral studies at the University of Iowa. A fellow student, Stan Zerlin, taught me a few chords on the guitar and I became devoted to folk music. Mixed in with my recordings of Josh White, Burl Ives, Richard Dyer-Bennet, and Leadbelly were two vinyl discs of Mark Olf singing Yiddish folk songs. I learned these and also studied Ruth Rubin's collection, *Jewish Folk Songs in Yiddish and English*. Eventually, with my wife, Eileen, and our friends Floyd and Fran Horowitz, we put on a concert of Yiddish music for the local Iowa City community.

It was many years before I again became occupied with Yiddish. In 1976, now with three children in tow, we went for the first time to Israel. I was on leave from the University of Minnesota for four months and was teaching at Tel Hashomer Hospital. My children had studied Hebrew in the Minneapolis Talmud Torah, and I was delighted (and surprised) to find that the two older children could converse, carry out transactions, ask for directions, and attend classes in Hebrew. My wife had won a Hebrew medal in New Utrecht High School and both of us had made efforts to learn some Hebrew in preparation for our trip, but we could utter only a few words of Hebrew before being drowned by the deluge that came back at us. In the *shikun* (housing complex) where we had an apartment there were neighbors who could speak half a dozen languages, but if English wasn't one of them, we were lost, cut off.

But not entirely. We discovered that some of the Yiddish that had swirled around us as children had lodged in our brains. We visited Eileen's uncle and aunt in Haifa for a long weekend and were bathed in Yiddish. I also discovered relatives—my grandmother's nieces and nephews—who had come to Israel from Europe or by way of South America. They saw my grandmother in my face, and I saw her in theirs. Our first encounter took place in the hospital ward where Bluma was recovering from eye surgery. Several of us gathered around her bed, excited by this family meeting, exclaiming with boisterous good will.

A nurse ordered us to keep it down, to remember there were other patients on the ward. We couldn't. Our joy and enthusiasm were too great. The nurse admonished us still again, harshly, and Bluma, in a Yiddish that I fully apprehended, said dismissively, "*Zey zaynen nit unzer Yidn!*" These are not our Jews!

Back in Minnesota after the sabbatical, I was caught up in family and work. Computers had invaded the academy and I was busy trying to master that language. Still, something in me had been stirred, and when I saw an announcement of an introductory course in Yiddish at the Minneapolis Talmud Torah, I signed up. Soon after, my colleague Maurie Kreevoy told me about the Yiddish Vinkl club that meets monthly. I dug out the old song sheets I had used in Iowa, collected them in a book, and now regularly lead our members in Yiddish song, adding new ones as I learn them.

With Maurie's encouragement I also learned to read Yiddish. We meet at the University Campus Club every Wednesday at noon to read to each other a text we've been working on at home. Diners at other tables, professors of chemistry, mathematics, Romance languages, come near to discover what exotic linguistic exercise we're engaged in, or to tell us that they had heard Yiddish in their youth. Laboriously, and with my Weinreich dictionary always at hand (now fallen apart and replaced with a hardcover version), I have been reading Peretz and Sholom Aleichem in the original, and we're slowly working our way through *East River* by Asch. It has been a thrill, a joy, a *farganigen*.

Now I, though still a learner, have become a teacher. After Shabbos services at Adath Jeshurun synagogue, I meet in the library with two other congregants who want to learn to read Yiddish, one younger than I and one older. My older student has an extensive vocabulary but never learned to read, and I have the joy of passing that skill along to him. And so in a modern, progressive, Conservative shul, Yiddish words join with the echoes of Hebrew and Aramaic once a week.

I did not teach Yiddish to my children. I came to it too late. They have studied French and Hebrew and Spanish. One of my grandchildren is so eager to learn Latin (which is not offered in her high school) that she's taking a course via the Internet. Clearly, my children and grandchildren love languages, but have lived in an environment where only a few Yiddish words are spoken. Still, they've learned some of my Yiddish songs, seen my awakening love of the language, and know that something special awaits them if they choose to follow the path I've been taking. When we're together I tease them with phrases designed to whet their curiosity, even as we do at the Passover seder.

"*Shtey glaykh*," my grandfather said. I loved him dearly. He saved my hide on more than one occasion by mending torn trousers so that the rips weren't visible. He helped turn away my mother's wrath. He fed my fantasy life by regaling me with plans for our trip to the Moon, just the two of us, long before there was a space program. "*Shtey glaykh*," he would say as I stood on a low bench and he crouched to mark where the cuffs should go. In those days, I thought "shtey glaykh" meant only, "Be still, don't move, stop wriggling or I'll stick you with these pins." But now I know better. Now I know he was telling me that as I grow into adulthood and find my way in the world, I should stay firm, remember my roots, be loyal to our traditions of study and learning, and that those traditions include the Yiddish language that has nourished and sustained our people for more than a thousand years.

# Happy Birthday, Mom

I DON'T RELISH VISITING New York in late August; it's likely to be punishingly hot and humid. But there was to be a gathering for Mom's 94th birthday, and though by this time Mom didn't much enjoy "celebrations"—the excitement, the pressure, the crowd of people—I, the older son, had to be among the well-wishers. Joel and Ann, my brother and his wife, offered to have something in their backyard. All the relatives would be there. It would be a good chance to see everybody, and without the blaring music that so often made it impossible to talk with anyone at the weddings and Bar Mitzvahs I'd attended in recent years.

There was a second reason for our trip. We were obliged to see and express enthusiasm for Mom's new home, an assisted living facility. She had been living on her own since Dad died, thirty-six years earlier. At first she remained on Seventy-seventh Street in Brooklyn. There she had to climb a steep, poorly lighted staircase to reach her second-floor apartment. Mr. Delvecchio, the landlord, was stingy with heat as well as electricity and the place was freezing in winter. And she'd had some personal unpleasantness with Mr. Delvecchio. He was not happy to have this elderly woman living in his building. If she were to leave, the apartment would no longer be rent-controlled and he could charge much more than she was paying.

After fifty years on Seventy-seventh Street, she finally moved, to a building on Bay Parkway, not far away, with an elevator and plenty of heat. Her new apartment was smaller, but she was comfortable there, got to know her neighbors, was close to shopping along Eighty-sixth Street, and also to her sister, my aunt Esther. She lived alone, and that was fine with her.

Of late, however, Mom had become increasingly frail and unsteady. She had a serious fall and broke her arm. To her dismay, Joel arranged to have live-in help, and a succession of dark-skinned women from different African countries stayed with her. The apartment had only one bedroom and the attendant seemed always to be in the way. Mom resented the constant presence of someone in her domain, especially when the someone cooked native dishes that Mom couldn't tolerate—not even the odors of the spices—and played loud, unfamiliar music throughout the day. It was a humiliation to live that way. But Joel insisted. She needed someone to look after her at least until her arm healed.

I had been gone from New York for many decades, so naturally the burden of care and decision-making fell on my brother. Joel was the one she summoned when she felt ill, had a doctor's appointment, an errand to run. He was always on call. The same week she broke her arm, Joel fell off a ladder trying to clean the gutters on his home and dislocated his shoulder. That time he asked me to come from Minnesota for a week to help out. He wasn't able to drive Mom to her doctor's appointments. Joel and I sat with her for long periods in the crowded orthopedist's waiting room and accompanied her when the doctor finally examined her. I marveled at her tolerance for pain as he manipulated her broken arm. She was more stoic than I.

After several weeks, she insisted that she was sufficiently healed to be on her own. She could no longer abide having strangers with her day and night. She and Joel worked out a compromise: She would promise to use her walker whenever she left the apartment—even if just to dispose of garbage—and she would accept daily visits from the attendants; but they would leave after helping her with dinner. She would have the evenings to herself.

That relative freedom didn't last very long. One morning, as she prepared to make her usual cup of coffee, the burner under the coffeepot didn't come on. The pilot light had gone out. Mom panicked. Rather than turn off the stove, she turned all the burners on, full blast. Fortunately, someone in the building smelled the gas, came into her apartment, and shut them off. The next day the building superintendent called Joel and reported what had happened.

"Something has to be done," he said. "She's a danger to herself and everyone else in the building."

Joel told Mom that the stove had to go. "You don't need it. All you do is make coffee once a day, and maybe cook an egg occasionally or heat up some soup."

He opened her refrigerator. "Look what you've got in here. You're getting kosher Meals On Wheels from Catholic Charities five days a week. You never finish the food they bring you." The refrigerator was full of unopened cartons of milk, most of them long out of date.

"And what about all these containers of applesauce, mushy peas, and pasta that you'll never eat and I can't convince you to throw away? You don't need a stove. I'll get you something better."

A few days later he bought Mom a microwave and showed her how simple and useful it would be. "Look, you just push a couple of buttons and in minutes the water for 'Instant' or tea is hot, or the soup's reheated. You'll love it once you get the hang of it."

He didn't understand. To make a real cup of coffee, she needed her ancient glass Pyrex that sat on a stove, with the metal basket and stem that the water perked through. "I don't want to get the hang of it. I don't want 'Instant.' I can't possibly make a cup of coffee in that thing."

She pleaded with Joel. "I'll be careful. It will never happen again. It was an accident, everyone has an occasional accident. I was preoccupied that morning, that's all. I… I was thinking you hadn't called in a long time."

"Mom, I call every day. Look, you have no choice. Unless the stove is removed or disabled, the landlord is going to evict you."

In the last few months, several of Mom's friends in the building had died or been moved by their children to nursing homes. It really wasn't the same old building any more. At about that time, a new assisted living facility was being built in Rockville Center, just minutes from my brother's home. It was bright and clean, with a dining room where Mom could take all of her meals. A nursing staff was always on the premises and there would be many programs for the residents. As one of the first residents, she could have her choice of rooms.

Joel persuaded Mom to look at the place. Why not have a fresh start in an attractive new facility where she could be on her own but still have all the care she needed? Mom was tormented by doubts. The decision to move was momentous. She would be leaving Brooklyn for the first time since the early years of her marriage. She would be separated from Uncle Meyer, who visited several times each week, often bringing groceries. She would no longer be doing her own shopping, meeting neighbors in the hallway while picking up the discount flyers. She would be leaving everything that was familiar to her and moving in with strangers.

I spoke with her on the telephone. "I know it's hard, Mom. But I agree with Joel that it's the right time. He can't keep running into Brooklyn for every little thing, and it's not safe for you to be living alone. I don't want something to happen to you."

"But I won't know anyone there. I don't even know if there will be any Jews. Who will I talk to? It will be so lonely. What if no one likes me?"

"Mom, you'll make friends. You always do. As soon as they get to know you a little bit, you'll be surrounded by friends. You never had trouble making friends."

"You really think it's the right thing?"

"I do, Ma. And right after you've moved in, we'll come out to visit you in your new home."

Our friends Floyd and Fran Horowitz were to be out of town that week and their apartment near the Natural History Museum and across from Central Park would be empty. They invited us to come early and have a few days in Manhattan before going to Long Island. On our trips to New York we rarely have time to do more than visit family. Now we'd be able to go to a museum, perhaps get tickets to a couple of plays, just walk the bustling streets of Manhattan.

Eileen and I had one evening and part of two days to strut around like tourists before receiving the telephone call from Joel. "You had better get out here. Mom is in the hospital. She spiked a fever and is very ill."

Within the hour we were in a cab heading for Long Island. The driver was speeding and was pulled over by a state trooper. "You going to a funeral?" he asked. I almost smiled.

We dropped our luggage at my brother's house and then went to the hospital. Mom was in great discomfort. A recurrence of pancreatic cancer. There was little that could be done for her. The hospital social worker advised that we contact hospice. We roamed the hospital floor trying to get the help my mother needed.

"Nurse, please, a bedpan."

"Nurse, please, remove the bedpan."

"Nurse, can she have some liquid?"

"Nurse, please, please, do something to relieve her pain."

Her groans were intolerable. I tried to comfort her, beguile her with stories of the children and grandchildren, but she was in too much distress to be comforted.

Mom was a proud woman, concerned about her appearance and how others evaluated her. It was painful to see her utterly dependent on others for her most basic needs, lying in her own urine until a nurse could be summoned. It was degrading. The nurses were always busy, attending to other patients or doing paperwork. Joel became angry, insistent, to little effect. I wanted the hospice care now, but it would take some time. It always takes time. Various forms would have to be filled out; we'd need to have papers signed. The social worker would begin the process.

Though there was nothing to be done but offer palliative care, the doctor ordered some tests, including an MRI. Mom protested. She didn't want any more tests, but she was wheeled out anyway, only to return soon after. She couldn't tolerate the procedures. As the day wore on, she was in constant pain. She scarcely knew we were at her bedside.

We returned to Joel's house for the night, and were awakened early with the news that Mom had died. The hospice arrangement never materialized. She was still in her bed when we arrived at the hospital. The mortician was on his way. I held her hand for a moment. We had only enough time to say a final goodbye before she was taken from us and brought to the funeral home.

Dad had bought gravesites for both of them many years ago and when he died a double stone was erected, one side blank, patiently awaiting the language that would mark my mother's reunion with him. In keeping with Jewish custom, the funeral was held quickly, less than forty-eight hours later. The rabbi who presided was hired by the chapel. He had never met my mother, but interviewed several of us before the funeral and based on these gleanings fashioned a eulogy that probably spoke more about us than Mom. We gathered at Joel's house afterward for *shiva* and received well-wishers there for the next three evenings.

During the day, Eileen and I helped Joel and Ann clear out the apartment in Brooklyn and also the assisted living facility. We gave some furniture to the superintendent and others in the building, and stuffed clothing and shoes in plastic bags to donate to charity. It was done hurriedly. There was no time to fondle items, reflect on their history. The apartment needed to be emptied. Eileen salvaged a set of dishes and silverware that she shipped home to Minnesota. I found a shoebox with photographs and letters, many from me. The photos were not in any order and were not identified or labeled. I took them back with me. Two years later, when I was emotionally ready to deal with them, I used the photographs to create a genealogy album that I shared with other family members.

We also had to empty Mom's room in the assisted living facility. The few items of furniture—a television set, some chairs, her new bed—we donated to the facility, though we kept a seder plate, a few knickknacks, and a purse filled with old coins.

In one of our visits to the facility, I met Mrs. Henderson, the supervisor who had welcomed Mom and tried to make her feel comfortable. She was a pleasant woman and full of regret at Mom's death.

"I really liked Mrs. Siegel," she assured me. "Your mother was shy and self-conscious at first," she said, "but I told her that she would be just fine. And I believe she would have. She was such a bright woman."

Mrs. Henderson went on to tell us that by the end of the second day Mom had already staked out a table in the dining room with people who enjoyed her company.

"Oh, and I have to tell you something very special," she added. "Wednesday is our bingo night. I knew your mother played mahjong and cards and I was sure she would enjoy bingo."

I smiled, recalling the boisterous pinochle and gin rummy games Mom and the rest of her family played Sunday mornings at Grandpa and Grandma's house. I also remembered that Aunt Esther almost always got the better of Mom in those games, and Mom was not a gracious loser—or perhaps it was that Esther was not a gracious winner.

Mrs. Henderson went on. "Your mother was reluctant to join the bingo group, but I told her that it would be fun. 'After all,' I told her, 'you don't have to win to have fun.'"

That brought another smile to my face. This kindly Mrs. Henderson hadn't had enough time to know Mom very well.

"We always have snacks after bingo, and I knew it was Mrs. Siegel's birthday. She didn't say anything, but I keep track of birthdays from the records. When we had snacks, I brought out a cupcake with a single candle on it. We all sang 'Happy Birthday.' I think she was pleased."

I imagined Mom being serenaded, trying to look pleased. Maybe, in this setting, she truly was.

"Oh, but the best thing," she continued. "Your mother was the biggest winner of the evening. She wiped everyone else out. It made such a difference in her feeling about being here. I could see it!"

That information gave me a big smile. Mom had a birthday celebration after all. And that triumphant bingo night, just days before her actual birthday, what a wonderful gift; surely better than anything we could have chosen for her. And Aunt Esther wasn't there to spoil it!

# There's Bears in There

JOSHUA, MY SIX-YEAR-OLD SON, was upset with me. "But Dad, you promised we'd go to the dump. You promised!"

"I know. I know. But it's raining and it's getting dark and we have to get ready to leave for home in the morning."

"But you promised!"

He was right. Years earlier, we had vacationed along the Gunflint Trail in northern Minnesota with Jane and Clark Starr, and they'd taken us to the local dump to see bears foraging in the garbage. Josh was too young to accompany us on that great adventure, but he had heard about it often enough. I'd promised that this time he, too, would see the bears, but the days had flown by and this would be our last chance.

"All right. But even the bears won't be out on a night like this."

David, Karen, and Josh climbed into the car. Eileen stayed behind to finish packing. The road was covered with branches from the storm and it was still raining. I wasn't certain I'd be able to see the sign to the dump in the waning light. Sure enough, I passed it and had to turn around. I drove slowly down the unpaved path toward the dumpsite. It was raining so hard we could barely make out the sides of the dump. It was also getting darker and I was worried we'd drive off the lip and get buried in garbage.

I inched forward. There were no bears. Josh was terribly disappointed. He got out of the car to get closer to the edge. Karen decided to stay behind and stay dry. Dave and I followed Josh. I held his arm to keep him back.

"Dad! I can't see anything. I just want to go a little closer."

"Josh, we're getting wet, and it's cold, and there are no bears. Let's get out of here."

There really was nothing to see. The car headlights barely cut the darkness and we could only make out the vague outline of a large pit. After a few moments I said, "Well, that's it. I told you there wouldn't be any bears in this kind of weather. Let's go back."

Josh was not ready to give up. "But Dad, can't we just…."

Just then there was a loud crack of thunder and the entire dump was lit up by lightning. Josh jumped. Fortunately, he jumped backwards. The lightning showed that he was at the lip of the crater, and close to falling in. We could see the entire dump and the heaps of garbage everywhere.

David and I turned towards the car, but not until we had a wondrous sight. Bears were feeding on garbage all around the dump, some close to where we were standing. A few of them saw us the same moment we saw them and turned their heads in our direction to get a better look at the interlopers.

Josh bolted for the car just as Karen was getting *out* of the car. "What's all the excitement?"

A second flash of lightning showed her only too clearly and she too dove for the car, with Dave and me right behind.

Josh, the brave one, the insistent one, now became the sensible one. "Let's get out of here, Dad. THERE'S BEARS IN THERE!"

I backed out slowly, unable to see the road in the dark, half expecting a bear to drape itself over the windshield, or to feel the car sliding over the edge in the mud. We reached the main road. We could hear the sounds of limbs cracking and falling around us. If we don't get eaten by a bear, I thought to myself, we'll be crushed by a tree. We made it back to the cabin safely and the children fell over themselves in their excitement to tell their mother what they had seen.

"One at a time, please," she said. "I can't make out a word of what you're saying. Your Dad was right, wasn't he? No bears!"

That remark started a fit of laughing among the children. Finally, Karen recovered long enough to say, "There's bears in there," and the laughing started again. Eileen looked at me, but all I could do was smile and chime in, "Yep. There sure were bears in there!"

The following morning the road was strewn with branches and we had to dodge puddles, but the skies were calm. We passed the entrance to the dump, now easy to see in the bright sunshine. No one suggested we stop. Instead, the children shouted, in unison, "THERE'S BEARS IN THERE!" and the giggling didn't stop until we had left the Gunflint Trail far behind.

# Where Are Joshua's Glasses?

JOSHUA SIEGEL IS ALMOST, but not quite, nine years old. His father often tells people that Joshua is nine. Then Joshua will correct his father. "Not exactly." Joshua frequently has to correct his father.

One day his father was impatient with Joshua: "Hurry up. Put on your coat. We're late for your appointment."

"Not exactly," Joshua corrected him. "We are going to be late, but we are not late yet." Joshua was right, of course, but his father would not admit it. Instead he rushed Joshua from the house.

Joshua wears eyeglasses. Well, not exactly. Joshua is supposed to wear eyeglasses. Most of the time they're either lost or in his pocket. Every morning Mr. Siegel cleans the smudges off Joshua's glasses. Joshua wears them for a few minutes but then he puts them in his pocket or his lunch bucket. Eyeglasses are a nuisance.

In the evening, Mr. Siegel comes home from work and says, "Joshua, why aren't you wearing your glasses?"

Joshua always answers, "They got smudged, so I put them in my pocket."

Joshua's father sighs a fatherly sigh and cleans them again. Mr. Siegel spends more time cleaning the glasses than Joshua does wearing them.

Some days Joshua takes off his glasses and can't remember where he put them. Then everyone in the family looks, but nobody can find them.

"Where did you put those glasses?" his father asks in that special voice he uses when he is annoyed.

Joshua throws up his hands and looks very innocent. "Don't ask me," he says. "If I knew where they were, I'd go get them."

One sunny afternoon Joshua climbed the tree in his front yard. When he reached the very top, he carefully placed his glasses on one of the branches so that they wouldn't get scratched. Later, when he came down from the tree, he forgot all about them.

That night, as usual, his father said, "Joshua, where are your glasses?" Joshua looked, but they weren't in any of the customary places. They weren't in any of his pockets, or his lunch bucket, or under his bed. They were nowhere.

Mr. Siegel became very annoyed. "Joshua, I am tired of always looking for your glasses. Every day you lose them."

"Not exactly," Joshua corrected his father. "I didn't lose them on Tuesday."

"But Joshua, on Tuesday they were still lost from Monday!"

"Still, I didn't lose them on Tuesday, and you said…"

His father walked away before Joshua could finish his sentence. Joshua thought that was very impolite, and his parents were always telling him to be polite.

Later that evening Aane came to play, but Joshua was still eating his soup (with a fork, because of the noodles), so Aane went outside to wait. He looked up into the tree and saw something bright and shiny on a high branch.

"Maybe it's a diamond ring," he thought, "or a tiny spaceship from another planet." He climbed the tree eagerly to find the treasure. When he got to the top he was very disappointed. It was nothing but Joshua's glasses. Aane slid down the tree and brought the glasses into the house. He pushed them at Joshua and said, "Here's your dumb old glasses." Everyone, except Aane, was quite happy that the glasses had been found.

Mr. Siegel said, "Joshua, please be careful not to lose these again."

Joshua corrected him. "I didn't lose them."

"Of course you did. We looked everywhere for them and still couldn't find them."

"But they weren't really lost. They were right in the tree where I left them."

His father forgot how happy he was to have the glasses back. His face was all twitchy and nervous.

"Joshua, I know they were in the tree. That's where you lost them. Aane found them. You lost them. They were lost! Lost! Lost!" His father was speaking in a much louder voice than Joshua would be allowed to use. Joshua was about to say, "Not exactly," but his father quickly left the room, making funny noises as he went.

It was a whole week before Joshua lost his glasses again. The search began once more. Joshua looked in all the rooms, under the couch, in his lunch bucket, but without success. He climbed the tree in front of his yard, not because he expected to find them there again, but because he felt it would be a good place to think things over for awhile. He didn't return until it was dark.

"Where have you been?" his father asked.

Joshua answered. "I've been thinking very hard about where I ought to look for my glasses."

They were nowhere to be found in the house, so Mr. Siegel called the neighbors that Joshua sometimes visited to ask if they had seen the glasses. No one had, but they all agreed to look carefully in their own homes. The neighbors immediately began to clean their living rooms, put away all their children's toys, dust under the beds, straighten the closet—all the while looking for Joshua's glasses.

They had no luck with the glasses, but Mrs. Efron recovered the purse she had misplaced on Mother's Day, and Mrs. Kortright found the earring she had been missing, and Mrs. Fosse found the puzzle piece everyone thought Oona had swallowed. Mrs. Glennon found two quarters under the couch and gave them as a reward to Joshua since, because of him, her house was now so neat and clean.

Joshua's father decided that the glasses had vanished from the earth, and so he bought Joshua a new pair. No sooner did he give them to Joshua than Mrs. Danielson called on the telephone. She was very excited. "I found them! They were stuffed into a couch cushion."

That had been Joshua's idea. He had put them in the cushion so that they wouldn't be crushed while he and Michael wrestled. He had been right, too. They hadn't broken, even though Mrs. Danielson had sat on them.

Now Joshua had two pairs of glasses, the old ones Mrs. Danielson had retrieved, and the new ones his father had bought. The first thing he did was to put the old pair in a very special hiding place that no one but he knew about. They would be safe there until he needed them. The new ones he put on his head. He promised his father he would be very careful with them from now on.

He truly was, but one day, after jumping into piles of autumn leaves and rolling down grassy hills and climbing over fences, he suddenly realized that his glasses had disappeared. It was very puzzling and mysterious. His father liked to read mystery books, but he didn't appreciate the real-life mystery right in his own home. When he discovered that Joshua wasn't wearing his glasses, he began to speak to him in a very loud voice that some would even call shouting.

"You did it again. You lost those glasses again. You are driving me crazy. I can't keep running out to buy you new glasses. They are expensive. They…"

Joshua waited until his father stopped to catch his breath. Then he said, "I remember where they are. I didn't lose them. They are in my lunch bucket. I know exactly where I put them."

His father felt silly for having scolded Joshua. He apologized and told Joshua, "Go get your lunch bucket and bring me the glasses. I'll clean them for you."

This was much more pleasant, but Joshua said, "I can't."

"What do you mean you can't? Just get the glasses like a good boy and bring them to me."

"I can't," Joshua repeated.

"But you just told me they're in your lunch bucket. So of course you can bring them to me."

"Not exactly," Joshua said. "I know they're in my lunch bucket, but I've lost my bucket."

Mr. Siegel was too upset to get more upset. "All right. They are lost. I'll order a new pair for you. In the meantime, go get the old ones and put them on."

Joshua was very proud of his father for being so sensible about it all. He went to get his old glasses. This time he would put them on and never let them out of his sight.

"Now let's see," Joshua thought to himself. "Where have I hidden those old glasses?"

Were they in the secret hiding place in the attic? No, he and Aane had made that into their clubroom. Perhaps in the ripped lining of his mattress? No, Mom had repaired that. Ahh! In the drawer with his socks. No, that wasn't it. Where could they be?

He congratulated himself. "Boy, I've really got a good hiding place. No one will find it. One thing is sure. Those glasses are not lost. No sir. They are safe and sound in my secret place. If only…If only I could remember where that secret place is."

*Exactly…*

# Piano Bentsh[1]

WE ALMOST SOLD THE PIANO. The children were gone, neither Eileen nor I play, and it takes up room. We considered giving it to Karen and Matt, but there was some question whether a piano that had so long been in the Midwest would survive the dry climate of Colorado. Dave's family already had a piano and Josh would have no use for it. To me, at least, it seemed best to sell it. Our friend Clare had expressed interest in taking lessons again. She looked at the piano and tentatively played a few chords. Then she returned with her teacher who tried it out and found it quite satisfactory. One key needed repair, but otherwise it was a good piano. We would sell it for slightly more than we'd paid for it.

The piano had arrived in our house when we weren't looking. I was on sabbatical at the time and the family to whom we rented our home, the Lovells, didn't merely move in. They took possession. On a return visit I stopped in and saw that they had rearranged all of the furniture, had taken our pictures off the walls and put up their own, and bought a piano so their children could continue lessons. At the end of the year they sold it to us. It came with a pedigree, official papers indicating that it had been built in Chicago by the Hamilton Company, an affiliate of Baldwin, in 1915, seven years before our house was built.

A piano would have been an incredible luxury when my brother and I were growing up in our small Brooklyn apartment. People with their own piano belonged in a different world. Uncle Meyer had a piano, but he also owned his home, a car, and a grocery store. Cousin

---

[1] In Yiddish, "bentsh" means to bless.

Paul had a piano, but it really was his wife's, and she came from a more highly educated and cultured background than did my kin.

Thanks to the Lovells, I now owned my own piano, in my own home in Minneapolis. I'm not sure which part of that last sentence is more remarkable. I grew up in a tiny New York apartment, sharing a room with my brother, surrounded by secondhand furniture. Other than personal effects my family never owned anything.

Several musical friends tried out our Hamilton piano and told me it had very nice tone. At social gatherings, one of our guests would sometimes play and I would enthusiastically sing along with others around the piano. Then they'd all go home and to my surprise the piano would still be there. The piano player hadn't taken it with him.

We arranged for our children to have piano lessons from Mrs. Titus. Josh, our youngest, abandoned his lessons early, but David and Karen gained proficiency. They gave annual recitals and participated in citywide competitions. David, in particular, had a flair and earned a certificate commending him for his musical expression.

I was the one agitating to sell the piano. I am always tediously fussing about simplifying our lives, about discarding unused objects, about putting things in the hands of people who would get some use out of them. What good is a piano that merely sits in a corner of the den, blocking the light, scarcely ever touched, when someone like Clare could be getting pleasure from it? This time Eileen agreed—right up to the moment we were to sell it, and then she couldn't do it. Too many memories. Too long a fixture in our house. Too much a part of us to part with.

Eileen was wise to overrule me. When the children and grandchildren visit, the piano gets a workout. Zachary, our youngest grandchild, loves to "play" and I tolerate the noise much more patiently than I did with our children. His older sister, Allison, thrilled me recently by picking out the melody to Beethoven's "Ode to Joy." Where did she hear that, in her rock 'n' roll family? David will occasionally play, sometimes together with one of his children. I have memories of Karen foraging in the piano bench for her old music (of course, we've kept it all) and playing a piece from her childhood. Best of all,

David's two children, Elana and Jacob, have been quite serious about their piano lessons and play music, real music. Jacob is very talented and has been composing pieces as well as playing jazz piano for the past several years. Not long ago Elana gave me my first piano lesson, gently guiding my fingers on the keys.

So, it's settled. The piano remains where it has been for the past forty-two years. But nothing is so settled that it can't be unsettled. Matthew recently called from Colorado. Zachary wants to take piano lessons. Matt has a friend in Boulder who can make any necessary adjustments or repairs to acclimate the piano to its Colorado home. These old pianos have much to recommend them and it would take thousands of dollars to buy a new one of comparable quality in Colorado. Matt has said he'll pay for the shipping.

*The scales have become unbalanced; the staff is in the other hand; the notes are flying off in all directions; everything is off bass; I treble with emotion when I think of it.*

Now I, who was so insistent that we give the piano away, am reluctant to part with it, and Eileen, who couldn't bear to see it go, is eager to send it to Colorado. She points out that we'll probably have to move into smaller quarters in the next few years, at which point the piano will probably have to go. Why wait, she argues, and end up giving our precious piano to a stranger when the children can use it now? Entirely logical, but she earlier convinced me that we should keep it, and I've adjusted to that idea, made it my own. Now I want to have it here when the children visit. I enjoy hearing them play in our home and I certainly don't want to think about moving. I want things to remain as they are.

How will it all turn out? Will we ship the piano to arid Colorado where the climate may take its toll, and Zachary may or may not sustain his interest in playing? Will we move, and if so, will we bring the piano with us? For the answer to these and other profound questions, stay tuned.

In the meantime, I offer a piano bentsh: *Dear God, bless this piano that has patiently, stoically, endured the attentions of our children and grandchildren. When they were young, their hands pounded indifferently* on its keys, and made a tumult. But as they matured, they learned to treat it with love, and their hands caressed it. And it has brought music and happiness to our home.

And let us sing, Amen!

# A Ring for Every Finger

"REPEAT AFTER ME," the rabbi said as Eileen and I stood under the *chupah* (wedding canopy) at the Benson Chateau in Brooklyn.

"With this ring, I thee wed…"

I slipped a plain gold band on her finger. Until that moment, Eileen's hands were unadorned. We had decided that we would not formalize our engagement with a diamond ring. We could scarcely afford it and, more to the point, we rejected such bourgeois status symbols. Of course, we were both very young. I was twenty-one, Eileen not quite nineteen in 1953.

I had been a friend of Eileen's brother Julius when he and I were students at New Utrecht High School, and I had often walked the few blocks from my family's apartment on Seventy-seventh Street, across the trolley tracks and under the El on New Utrecht Avenue, to visit Julius at his home. Eileen was the invisible little sister then. Julius and I lost track of each other when we went to different colleges, but we met up again on the BMT subway line one evening. Julius had taken Eileen as his "date" to a dance at City College, and I was coming home from the night shift at Reuters, in Manhattan. We rode the train together and exited at the same Seventy-ninth Street station. Eileen was beautiful and captivating, and not long afterward I overcame my shyness and called her.

We dated for two years, parted for one summer while I was a counselor at Camp Wel-Met, and began again even more earnestly when I returned. We were never formally engaged. I didn't ask for her hand, and I didn't petition her father for permission to marry her. However, one weekend afternoon when I came to call for Eileen, her parents sat me down and put a record on the phonograph. It was Sophie Tucker singing, "Mr. Siegel, please make it legal, for me." The wedding plans began soon after. We left the sometimes troubled negotiations about the size and shape of the wedding ceremony to our parents, but on the matter of the rings we asserted ourselves. Instead of an engagement ring, I gave her a simple watch.

We moved to Iowa City in 1954 so that I could begin my graduate studies at the University of Iowa, and, one year later, signed on as host and hostess for the large old home that served as the Hillel House, a gathering place for Jewish students. In exchange for our efforts, we were given a small, rent-free apartment on the second floor.

Eileen's parents had come to the United States separately, in their teens. Her father, Jack, entered the country circuitously, after a stay in Cuba, and somehow found his way to New York, penniless and with no command of English. He became a house painter. Eileen's mother, Rose, had fled the Old Country to escape her stepmother, who was her own age, and intolerable. She moved into her sister's home and cared for her sister's small children. Jack was hired to paint the sister's house. They met, and married. Rose went to work as a seamstress in her brother-in-law's factory. Although Jack's work was seasonal and unpredictable, they managed to save. They bought the building they lived in, with a shop and an apartment below that they rented out.

It pained them that their only daughter didn't have an engagement ring. One day we received a package at the Hillel House from Eileen's parents, but instead of the usual emergency rations, it contained a ring—a diamond ring. I must admit I did not appreciate this gift. I grumbled that we could have made better use of the kosher salami they usually sent and if Eileen was to have an engagement ring, it should have come from me, not her mother and father.

Eileen, it turned out, was considerably more tolerant of bourgeois status symbols than I had understood. She slipped the ring on her finger and delighted in the play of light and color. Her pleasure was short-lived, however. Within a few weeks, and before we managed to get the ring insured, it vanished. We searched everywhere, but it was gone. We will never know what happened, but my guess is that Eileen removed the ring to wash up in the communal kitchen or in the bathroom—the ring was a bit too large—and it either fell into the sink or into the possession of one of the many students who trooped through the facility throughout the day and into the evening. The ring was never found and we never spoke of it to Eileen's parents.

The pain of losing the ring was mitigated somewhat because Eileen knew she would eventually inherit her mother's diamond ring. But there was more bad luck in store. Burglars managed to sneak up a flight of creaky stairs, into the second-floor Brooklyn apartment where Sophie Tucker had sung to me, and to walk off with all kinds of valuables. In fact, it happened twice. Included among the losses were valuable old coins, a collection of pocket watches, and Eileen's mother's diamond ring. This second ring had great sentimental value, and even I mourned its loss.

Do calamities truly come in threes? "You see this ring?" my mother would often say, extending her hand for Eileen to admire. "When I'm gone, this diamond is going to be yours!" My mother lived on the fourth floor of an apartment building on Bay Parkway, in Brooklyn. Many of the tenants, like my mother, were widowed and elderly. A man wearing a plumber uniform and carrying a tool box appeared at my mother's door one day and announced that he had just repaired a leak in the apartment above and was checking to see whether she had a problem too. In my family we were always impressed by workmen, because we had no mechanical skills and our only tools were a toy hammer and a bent screwdriver. The plumber carefully ran his hands along the wall over her kitchen sink, muttered to himself, and wiped his hands on his overalls. He noticed that my mother was wearing a diamond ring.

"Better put it in this glass," he advised. "It may have become contaminated from the leaking water." My mother, trusting and cooperative, complied.

"Oh, and would you check with your upstairs neighbor to see whether there is still any water dripping while I examine the pipes here?" Of course my mother would oblige the nice young man who had come, unbidden, to help her.

Dotty, in the apartment above my mother's, said, "What leak? I never had a leak." My mother turned white and raced back to her own apartment. The door was open, the "plumber" was gone, and so was my mother's—Eileen's—diamond ring. My mother was crestfallen. She could not forgive herself. She castigated herself for being gullible, stupid, and a thousand other things, none of them complimentary.

Eileen, when she heard, was also crestfallen. This was beyond coincidence. She had lost three diamond rings. It felt like a curse. Soon she began wearing rings on all of her fingers—inexpensive rings that looked like they'd come from a cereal box. One size fits all. Secret compartment. Hidden mirror that allows you to see around corners. Fake diamonds, emeralds, rubies. She was grieving.

For her sixtieth birthday, I finally bought Eileen a ring—not a diamond, but a tourmaline, her birthstone. At first she wouldn't wear it. She was sure something dreadful would happen to it, and so it sat in a vault. I persuaded her to wear it. The stone did fall out, but the jeweler from whom I'd bought the ring replaced the tourmaline at no charge. Perhaps the curse had been lifted.

Eventually, I gave a diamond ring to Eileen. For many years I worked in the Department of Communication Disorders at the University of Minnesota. Sharon, a colleague in the same department, became a close friend. We shared family stories and confidences. I rejoiced with her when her son became engaged to be married, and then commiserated when the engagement was called off. Sharon told me that the diamond engagement ring her son had given his fiancée had passed back and forth between them as their relationship altered, and had come to rest with her son, who was anxious to be rid of this symbol of all that had gone wrong. I sought to comfort Sharon with the tale of Eileen's disappearing rings. Sharon looked at me for a long moment.

"Why don't you buy my son's ring for Eileen? He's willing to sell it for less than he paid. It's a beautiful ring and Eileen will love it. I can bring it in for her to look at. She can take it to the jewelry store where it was bought to confirm its value."

"Sharon," I said, "With our history, the ring will probably be lost or stolen before I get it home."

"Nonsense," Sharon said. "You show it to Eileen and see if she's interested."

Eileen was interested. The ring was beautiful. It felt odd to own an engagement ring that had been destined for a different person, but on the other hand we knew we could give it a good home where it would be cherished. So the deal was consummated and the ring became truly Eileen's, molded to her finger and to her heart. She wears it still.

Now Eileen feels that it would be nice to have a second diamond ring. For a brief moment we thought there might be a prospect. Sharon's son recovered from the trauma of his broken engagement, and not long afterward he became engaged again. And then unengaged again. The young man was having the same luck with engagements that we had been having with rings. I knew there was now another homeless diamond ring, and I waited expectantly, but Sharon never mentioned it and neither did I. That's just as well. Her son has since made it all the way through still a third engagement, with another diamond ring, and is now married. The curse has been lifted for him, too.

You see, even with the stock market bouncing around, and unemployment much too high, and the international scene uncertain at best, and the environment in constant danger, and families falling apart in front of our very eyes—even in these freighted times, some stories have a happy ending.

# A New Silk Coat

MY WIFE IS DELIGHTED when I buy new clothes. Even when we were first married and were impoverished students at the University of Iowa, she fussed about my clothes. When it comes to my wardrobe, she immediately is drawn to the most expensive suit or trousers on the rack.

"Just try it on," she'll insist. "You don't have to buy anything. I just want to see how it looks on you."

If the price tag is enough to make me suck in my breath, you can bet her next response will be, "Perfect. It was made for you."

It's not that I don't like nice clothes. But I don't have patience for shopping, and I don't like the idea of spending big bucks for wide lapels when my suit with the narrow ones still fits perfectly well if I wear the trousers a little low on the waist. I don't approve of buying something just because "that's what they're wearing."

The other evening we were invited to dinner with some friends, and four of the men showed up wearing exactly the same camel-hair sports coat. The host had his in the closet. One of the men told me that in his law office one of the partners is assigned to shop for clothes for all of the attorneys. He picks out their clothes! Can you imagine? There are a lot of things wrong with being a college teacher, but at least I got to pick out my own clothes. With the aid of my wife, Eileen, of course.

These days I mostly shop by myself at some nice men's store—when they're having a sale. I get to know one of the salesmen and let him decide what looks good on me. The salesman really becomes a stand-in for my wife. Several months ago Belleson's sent their annual announcement of THE BIG SALE—50 percent off almost everything.

Eileen was delirious with anticipation. We had to go to Belleson's to see if there was something on sale that was just right for me.

When we got there, the 42-long section was filled with a dazzling collection of suits and coats. I couldn't begin to sort through them, but with uncanny instinct Eileen immediately zeroed in on a shimmering blue sports coat with pearl buttons and a subtle dark blue thread mingled among the pale blues. She urged me to try it on. It felt wonderful, soft and silky—absolutely elegant. And absolutely the only coat in the entire section that wasn't on sale. The price tag for the jacket was more than I had ever spent for a suit, even when it came with a vest and two pairs of pants, as in the old days. I was flabbergasted, but that just set my wife's jaw. That jacket was made for me. It would be a cruel to leave it behind. The transaction was consummated on the spot. The 50 percent sale was forgotten. As the British say, I had taken silk. I walked out of the store with a lovely silk coat that hadn't even needed alterations.

I was taught as a child that the first thing one does with something new is to put it away so that it stays new. That's what I did with my silk coat until Eileen finally talked me into wearing it to work. I have to admit I did get quite a few compliments. However, arrangements that seem to be made in heaven sometimes go awry. It was an accident, pure and simple, and not the only time I had done such a dumb thing. I put my felt-tip pen—my black felt-tip pen—in my inside jacket pocket, where I always put it. The pen was new and fresh with possibilities. It was also fresh with dark, black, indelible ink. I knew something was wrong when I returned home and saw my wife's horrified expression as I removed my outer coat. The ink had soaked into the pocket, through the lining, and onto the fabric of the lapel. Eileen looked at the disaster, mute and amazed.

The next morning I brought the jacket to my favorite cleaning store, but the store had just changed hands and Dick, the former owner, who had never in fifteen years done more than grunt to me, was gone. I showed the new owner the ink spot. "I'll do what I can," he said. Alas, he did too much.

Dick was a grunter, but also a cleaner. He knew his trade and his limitations. The new guy bought the store, but not Dick's knowledge or experience. When the jacket came back, the black spot had grown so that it now covered a huge area rather than just the pocket. I was defeated, ready to admit that silk coats that are not on sale are not for college professors. I would hang it in my closet as a personal reminder of the evils of materialism. Perhaps I would be able to wear it at a convention, with a name tag over the spot. Mostly, I wanted that coat out of my sight.

Eileen was not so quickly defeated. She marched into the cleaning store with my jacket and demanded to know what had happened. The new owner and his assistant got into a fight about which of them was responsible. She cut them off and let them know she didn't care which of them was the genius, but she intended to get the jacket repaired and would be back with the bill. She found a weaver who suggested taking a swatch from the underside of the uncontaminated lapel and weaving it around the pocket, a kind of organ transplant or bypass operation.

Several weeks passed. They were happy weeks because the jacket was out of sight and the fabric pathology report had not yet been delivered. When the day of reckoning came, it was—well, not bad, not at all bad. The weaving was beautifully done. There was no sign of the ugly black ink spot. The fabric was again soft and silky. The only problem was that it was a bit thin in the lapel. If I thrust my chest out too far, the underside of the lapel would show as bare, but who was I to thrust out my chest, a *schlemiel* like me? As far as I was concerned, a miracle had been wrought, and I was happy to put the coat back in my closet.

Eileen wasn't quite finished. She went back to the cleaner as she had promised. The owner grimaced when he saw the bill, grimaced again when he saw Eileen's expression, and paid up, in full.

I have now found another cleaning store a few blocks away. I haven't given the new cleaner the critical test. I haven't brought in my blue silk jacket. I don't wear it often and I'm not anxious to get it cleaned. It sits in my closet. I like it there. One of these days, on a really special occasion, I'm going to wear it again. I just have to remember not to puff out my chest.

# Laundry Day

I'M BEGINNING TO FEEL that I'm jinxed. The washing machine broke down last weekend. It wouldn't go into the spin cycle and the water wouldn't drain. Just a couple of weeks earlier, the refrigerator broke down beyond repair and had to be junked. The water softener went out too; the replacement is sitting in a box in the backyard, waiting to be installed. None of these appliances are mine. I've been subletting while on sabbatical in California this past year.

The refrigerator went first. One afternoon it let out a loud *CLUNK*. At first I thought it was my imagination, but when the ice cubes began melting and the ice cream formed a glob on the bottom of the freezer compartment I knew something was seriously wrong. It took half a dozen calls before I located a repairman who would come out the following morning.

After a cursory examination, the repairman replaced a relay and told me my worries were over. But that evening I was sure I heard another loud clunk, after which the refrigerator became ominously quiet. Though it was after working hours, I felt I ought to call the repairman again—I had already restocked the ice cream. He came from across town, took another look, and assured me the refrigerator had simply gone into its periodic defrost cycle. I was shamefaced. I had never had such a quiet refrigerator before. I offered him a cup of coffee and some ice cream. Though the hour was late, he charged me only a standard service fee and we parted amicably.

I rose the next morning to find the refrigerator in terminal defrost mode. The freezer was shedding ice-cream tears. The repairman returned once again to underscore the obvious—the refrigerator was dead. He didn't charge me for the call and I didn't offer him any ice cream.

I contacted the owners and they told me to buy a new refrigerator. Problem solved—though I experienced a degree of residual guilt about the expense. The lovely Santa Barbara winter had pretty well assuaged that feeling when the washer conked out. It didn't clunk, but it smelled like rubber was burning.

Was this to be my punishment for fleeing the Minnesota winter? The repairman—a new repairman—made a few minor adjustments and replaced a filter on the hot water hose before pronouncing the machine "fit." He gave it an affectionate pat on the way out.

But in a few days the washing machine had a relapse. I couldn't bring myself to tell the landlord another appliance had broken, so I developed a "work around," manually advancing the dial to the second rinse and wringing out the clothes by hand before putting them in the dryer. The dryer was working just fine, by the way. When that procedure got old I finally called the repairman back—the second repairman. (The first repairman I don't ever want to see again, though he was a very pleasant fellow.) Probing the machine more deeply, he came up with a pair of panties that had slipped down between the drum and the lid and wrapped itself around the axle. He didn't charge me for the second visit because he felt he should have done a better job of identifying the problem in the first place. Fair enough. He stayed to chat for awhile and we had a few chuckles about how those panties might have gotten entangled like that. He had a glass of lemonade although he wouldn't sit down. I didn't pass the bill along to the landlord.

Less than twenty-four hours later the bathtub backed up and soaked the bathroom floor. This was getting ridiculous. This time I called Kenny, the plumber recommended by the landlord in case of emergency. By now every problem felt like an emergency. Kenny couldn't get away immediately, but suggested I pour a gallon of cheap bleach down the drain. It worked. I mopped up around the bathtub and the hallway leading to the washer, concentrating my positive energy on the thought that all of my problems were now over. I had learned this technique

# LAUNDRY DAY

from my new California friends, but had not yet mastered it, to judge from the fact that the next morning there was a puddle of water around the washing machine again and the nice wooden tiles in the hallway were starting to buckle. The tiles had been a gift to my landlord and his wife from their children. I could see these lovingly cared-for tiles floating away in a flood for which I was somehow responsible, and I started to panic. It was Sunday and I wasn't sure whom to call. I had vowed never to call the first repairman again; the second one didn't leave his home number. That left Kenny.

I paced the floor. It was 7:00 a.m., not a decent time to call a plumber, even in an emergency. I waited until 9 before calling. Kenny arrived a few hours later and treated me with the sensitivity of a social worker. He had read the panic in my voice.

Kenny diagnosed the problem in a minute. One of the hose connections to the washing machine wasn't firmly in place. It had been leaking ever since the repairman had replaced the filter. Perhaps it jiggled loose when he pushed the machine back to the wall. Kenny cinched it up tight and the leak was stopped. That's all it took.

I mopped up the remaining water. The tiles stayed in place although they did darken a bit in the area near the washing machine. Or maybe they were darker all along and I hadn't noticed.

I'm happy to report that nothing else has broken down. Nothing will. I'm applying positive energy to guarantee that. Still, I don't use the washing machine. I have great faith in positive energy but while the washer was out of commission, I discovered a convenient launderette in the neighborhood and I've been bringing my clothes there. I like launderettes. When I was a teenager I worked in one for a summer in Brooklyn and enjoyed being surrounded by machines churning and whirling. I've been bringing my clothes to the launderette early in the morning when there aren't too many people. I bring a book and enjoy the tranquility while someone else's machine does the work. I don't worry about hoses or timers or motor belts. I just sit and read. It's a very secure feeling.

Besides, I get to meet some nice people at the launderette. Last week I met a very pretty, friendly woman and she put her clothes into the machine right next to mine though there were others she might have chosen. I don't know yet if she's married or otherwise attached but perhaps I'll find out next Tuesday. Tuesday is my laundry day.

# Visiting Day

DEBORAH KATZENBAUM'S GRANDMOTHER had been languishing in the Quality of Life Nursing Home for several years. Debbie had not really forgotten Bubbe Esther, but of late her grandmother often failed to recognize even her own children and was as likely to shrink from Debbie as to greet her. Debbie found the unpredictability of the old woman's behavior upsetting and had stopped visiting.

On her fortieth birthday, however, Debbie began to muse about her origins and where her journey would take her for the rest of her life. Her children were approaching their teens without serious impairment. Bernard, the youngest, was a difficult child, but no worse than many other children his age that other families were grappling with. She and her husband, Bert, had endured the first chaotic decades of their marriage and would soldier on, though Bert could not be counted on to understand her current restiveness. Debbie might also have wished they had become better off financially by this stage in their life together. They owned their own home, advertised as a "handyman's delight," but her husband was no handyman; vacations required careful planning and scrimping and so they took few; the kitchen had yet to be remodeled; both cars were old and neither was entirely reliable. They would somehow put the children through college, but private schools were unthinkable. As the children grew older, Debbie thought of going back to work, but to return to teaching would mean first returning to college to be recertified and she doubted she had the patience to be a student again. They managed. They lived within their means.

Debbie was not depressed as her fortieth birthday neared. She had no sympathy for women who made a big deal of going from one decade to another, but she did find herself becoming more reflective as she approached "middle age." A few generations earlier, forty would have been considered the twilight of many people's lives.

Debbie wanted to explore this new territory, to reflect on how she had gotten here, and to prepare for what lay ahead. It was in this mood that she felt the urge to visit Bubbe Esther. Old people, with their dim vision, can sometimes see ever so clearly into the past, where the blueprints for the future are hidden.

Much to her mother's surprise, Debbie announced that she intended to bring the children to visit their great-grandmother in the home.

"Why this sudden interest in Grandma?" her mother asked. "It has been at least a year since you last visited her."

"I know. I haven't been good. I've been too preoccupied. But I feel like talking with her. Everything seems so complicated now. Half the words we speak have hidden meanings. Everything seems to stand for something else. I want to know if the world was always this crazy."

Her mother shook her head. "Debbie, I don't understand half of what you are saying, but if you think that visiting your grandmother will bring you wisdom, you'll be disappointed. What you'll find instead are old and sick people who are often not aware of what's going on in front of their noses. But if you want to go, please do. Just don't expect too much. And if you wish, I'll go with you."

"No. Not this time. I'll go alone, with the children."

Bernard complained when he learned of their planned trip. "Aw, Mom, last time she didn't even know we were there. She just sat in her wheelchair and stared. It's boring. And the place stinks."

His sister Rebecca reassured him. "Old people are cool, Bernard. It's like there's another person inside them. You've just got to find it underneath all the wrinkles and stuff."

When they arrived at the home, they found Bubbe Esther staring into empty space as Bernard had predicted. Debbie hesitated for a moment, but then greeted her grandmother cheerfully.

"Hello, Bubbe. How are you? It's me, Debbie. And I've brought the children to visit you." She pushed the children in front of her. "Say hello to your great-grandmother, children."

The children jostled for a place directly in front of the old woman, but she made no response and showed no sign of recognizing them. Bernard wandered off.

"Don't they look grown-up?" Debbie asked her grandmother. "Don't you like Becca's hair like that? Mother said she looks like pictures of you when you were her age."

The elderly woman inclined her head towards Debbie, tried to fix her eyes on her, to understand what Debbie was saying. Suddenly she shrieked. Bernard had come around the back of the wheelchair and released the brake. The chair lurched forward.

"Bernard!" his mother exclaimed. "What are you doing? You'll frighten her to death. What's gotten into you?"

Bubbe Esther was indeed frightened and had begun to tremble. Debbie was distraught. Why had she come? Why had she brought the children? This was foolishness, a terrible idea.

"I'm sorry, Bubbe," she said. "He is forever doing things like that. I don't know what to do with him. I'm so sorry. We'd better go now. I had so many questions, and I wanted the children to hear you, but we had better go now, before something else happens." She clutched Bernard's hand and pulled him out of the room.

Rebecca remained behind. She reached out tentatively and began to stroke her great-grandmother's arm.

"Please don't feel bad, Bubbe. Bernard didn't mean anything bad. Mother says he is driving her crazy. He is always doing mischief. Mother said you understand a lot of things about life that we all should listen to, especially about the old days, when the world wasn't so crazy."

Rebecca's voice was soothing. The old woman peered at her and then, in a croak more than a voice, she said, "I don't know about old days or new days. In this place, all the days are the same."

Rebecca smiled broadly, delighted that she had coaxed some words from the old woman. "But the days are not all the same, Bubbe Esther. Today is visiting day, we came to visit."

Before the old woman could answer, Debbie returned. "Becca, I've been waiting for you in the car. Bernard is impatient to go home."

"I've been visiting with Bubbe Esther. She was talking with me but now I think she fell asleep. She likes me. I'd like to come back and visit again."

"Yes, yes, but now we have to go home. You know how impossible Bernard becomes when he's overwrought. We really must leave now."

As she spoke, Debbie took one last look at the woman in the wheelchair, dozing quietly, and for the first time during the visit she recognized her as the woman with the large embrace who had rocked her when she was hurt or unhappy. Bubbe Esther had been the soother, the protector who sometimes stood between Debbie and her own parents, who used to pull Debbie's face to her lips with two strong hands. She turned softly so as not to wake the old woman, and took Rebecca's hand. They left quietly.

It had rained and the air outside the home smelled fresh. Bernard was nowhere in sight and for a moment Debbie panicked. As she approached the car, Bernard suddenly pulled himself up from behind the wheel and pressed the horn. He grinned at his mother.

"Hey, Mom, look at me. I'm driving."

"Into the back seat, where you belong, and don't forget your seat belt. I don't know whether to be furious with you or grateful for getting your Bubbe to notice us."

"You're not mad, Mom? It was an accident. I didn't know the chair would start rolling."

"Bernard, you knew full well you were releasing the brake."

"Well, maybe, but I didn't think it would roll so far, or that Bubbe would react so strongly. Anyway, I'm glad I came. It wasn't so bad after all."

Rebecca added, "I'm glad I came, too. I didn't mind that place at all. I think I may decide to be a nurse, and work in places like where Bubbe is."

Debbie started the car. "That's nice, Rebecca, you be sure to tell that to your great-grandmother the next time you see her."

"When will that be?"

"Why, next visiting day, of course," her mother said.

# Driving Lessons

UNCLE MEYER AND UNCLE ABE drove Pontiacs, always Pontiacs. They loved cars and could tell the make and year just from hearing a car drive by. Sometimes, when Uncle Meyer parked in front of my house on Seventy-seventh Street in Brooklyn, I would climb in his car and pretend to drive, turning the wheel, peering ahead, sliding down so I could reach the pedals. That was grand fun, until Uncle Meyer came out and discovered that I had flooded the car by pressing on the gas pedal. Once Uncle Meyer took me for a ride and let me hold the steering wheel from the passenger seat next to him. I did it for a moment, then turned the wheel too sharply and became frightened when the car veered. It would be a long time before I learned to drive myself.

My family never owned a car. We never owned anything except personal belongings in our rented apartment. Even the stove and refrigerator were the landlord's. My grandparents didn't drive either. To everyone's surprise, Uncle Ben, Tante Chaika's second husband, bought a car in his advanced years. He left a twenty-dollar bill on the seat beside him while he was taking his road test and passed the test. Later, he offered to show me how well he could drive. We jolted, lurched, and bumped along. Drivers in other cars honked angrily at him as he strayed from lane to lane, but he interpreted their honking and waving as salutations and congratulations and waved and honked back cheerfully. He outlived Tante Chaika, married again, and died of natural causes.

Cars were still rare in Brooklyn during the 1930s and '40s when I was growing up. If they were parked strategically, the front or rear fender could stand for first or third base during punchball games (the sewer was second); and many was the young child who was encouraged by his parent to water the tires of a parked vehicle, rather than make a dash for a second floor apartment bathroom. We didn't need a car. A bus ran along Eighteenth Avenue and our apartment was just two blocks away from the Seventy-ninth Street station on the BMT line. We could travel to Coney Island by trolley or train. The trolley was slower but more satisfying. It was closer to the passing scenes, and it swayed back and forth with a rhythm that was a promise of the waves at the beach. And there was often excitement. Children—not me—would climb onto the back of the trolley and cling to it, hitching a ride and flirting with danger, either from the conductor or from the chance they would fall.

I completed three college degrees before I finally learned to drive, in Iowa City, Iowa. I finished my graduate studies in 1957 and was offered my first teaching job in Fargo, North Dakota. We decided to buy a car before we left Iowa, and also a trailer to haul our belongings. I bought a 1948 Studebaker—a model that looked the same from the front and the back. Floyd Horowitz volunteered to teach me to drive. Before he let me turn the key, however, Floyd announced that I should have a basic knowledge about automobiles and how they work. So he told me many things about carburetors and pistons and combustion, but I wasn't paying much attention. Now that I could reach the pedals, and had my own car, I was impatient to be driving. I took my PhD final examination and my driving test in the same week, and at the end of that week I was a doctor of philosophy, but not of driving. The following week I tried again and passed the exam, but not until I had put a significant dent in the side of my car practicing parallel parking.

No matter, the trailer was rented and loaded, I had a map that showed the way to North Dakota, I knew where the gas tank was, and I had a pretty good idea which was the brake pedal and which the clutch.

On the day we were to leave, Frances Horowitz appeared at our door with a sack full of sandwiches and a proposition.

"How about if I come along and help with the driving?" she said. "I can return to Iowa City by train."

"That's awfully nice of you. Are you sure?"

"Of course," she said. "I'll enjoy the break. How about if I do the first shift?"

"Sure," I said. "I'll take over when you get tired."

We drove a couple of hours and then stopped for coffee. I offered to take the next shift but she said, "I'm feeling fine. Why don't I go just a little farther." We stopped once or twice more, and she always suggested that she should drive just a little farther.

She drove straight through to Fargo, and never gave up the steering wheel until we had gotten to the train station. Then she bid us farewell, and I finally had the driving to myself. I moved the seat back, looked into the rearview and side view mirrors, gently let out the clutch, and was on my way, quite smoothly. I pulled into a parking lot a few moments later to ask directions. I was concentrating on driving the car and forgot about the trailer. I got the nose of the car into the lot and was driving very carefully and slowly as I looked for a possible parking space. Floyd Horowitz would have been proud of me. I almost made it, but then heard a very unpleasant sound as the wooden arm that had automatically been raised when I pulled the ticket from the dispenser got impatient, came down on the trailer, and was broken off as I inched my way into the lot.

That was the beginning of my real education as a driver. Eventually I taught my three children to drive, and each became a better driver than me. Like my friend Frances, when we travel together they invariably volunteer "to do the first shift." I offer to pitch in when they get tired. They never get tired.

# Teacher's Roll: Scenes from a Lectern

I WISH I COULD REMEMBER the names of all the students I've taught over the years, but I'm terrible with names. People who forget names are supposed never to forget a face, but not me. I forget everything—the name, the face, the context. Occasionally this leads to extravagant fantasies. I was captivated one day by the appearance of a young woman I saw while hurrying to my car in a pouring rain. Her bright red hair was hanging loosely and the rain was flowing down her face. Her image was hauntingly familiar and I stood in the rain wondering what part of my life she had belonged to and whether it was she I recognized or someone from my past that she evoked. I saw her once or twice more on campus and had the same immediate sense of recall, but I simply could not place her. Months later I was showing family slides, moving from birthday parties to summer vacations, when she materialized on the screen, wearing a green bathing suit that contrasted with her long red tresses. Her hair was wet and streaming as she patiently positioned my young son in the water and gave the signal to the speedboat. She was the waterfront instructor at the Isle O'Dreams resort in northern Minnesota.

Some names remain with me, even from my childhood. Mrs. Silver was my first grade teacher in 1938, the year I had to be hospitalized with osteomyelitis in my foot. I recall the lilting name of a girl I dated just once when I was a teenager in Brooklyn. Emily Gniatkowsky it was, and she lived in Greenpoint. Such a wonderfully melodic name. I remember some students, I'm sure, out of sheer vanity. Kathy Sceli sent me a note written in a fine, tight script, in green ink, in which she blessed me for my inspiration and special kindness. I don't recall any special kindness I did to deserve her blessing, but I kept her note. She too had red hair.

I also remember students who were less flattering. Mrs. Gonzales was short, gray, and plump. She stopped me after class to scold me.

"You talk too fast and you don't pronounce carefully," she said.

"I'm sorry, Mrs. Gonzales. It must be my New York background. I'll try to speak more carefully."

"It takes me longer to understand because I'm still learning English, and I'm not so young. My children don't have trouble, but I still think about the words."

"Why did you choose this class, Mrs. Gonzales?"

"I had to. I need it for graduate school."

Mrs. Gonzales in graduate school? She was an average student in a competitive program that rejected nine of every ten applicants. I should, perhaps, have returned to the topic at hand—my lecture style—but I had an image of this woman being pushed into a field where she would have only the remotest chance of success.

"Mrs. Gonzales, do you know how hard it is to get into graduate school in communication disorders? I think you may have gotten bad advice."

She was not perturbed. "I'll tell you who advised me, and you tell me if it was bad advice. One night I was sleeping and a voice woke me up. It told me to go to college and study speech therapy so I can help my people. I thought, how can I go to college? I never been to college. And I don't know anything about speech therapy. But then I came to Minnesota, and I got into college, and I found out about speech therapy. It's a miracle, right? It's all a miracle. So that's where I got my advice. What do you think?"

I was at a loss. Mrs. Gonzales saw my discomfort and smiled. Then she looked toward heaven.

"You know, God, come to think of it, that miracle is kind of old. Don't you think it's time to make another miracle for me?"

Mrs. Gonzales passed my course with a solid C grade. That was years ago. I hope she is doing speech therapy somewhere.

# TEACHER'S ROLL: SCENES FROM A LECTURN

It's not always the brightest students who succeed. Mrs. Gonzales had determination. So did Janet. Her classmates in Fargo were sophisticated, fashionably dressed sorority members and campus queens. By comparison, Janet seemed unfinished. She was very tall and very quiet. On the rare occasions when she spoke, she blushed, and her Scandinavian brogue rivaled my Brooklyn accent. Her spelling and grammar were atrocious. I had little hope for her. Still, she was persevering. She mutely accepted my criticism, and wrote and rewrote papers. One afternoon she appeared in my office and announced she had something to tell me. I feared she had finally had enough and intended to drop out of school.

"It's about your lectures," she said.

"Yes?"

"I don't see why you use those words when you lecture."

I was becoming irritated. Earlier that day, another student had upbraided me for teaching about the evolution of the vocal system. He didn't believe in evolution. "It's an established scientific thesis," I told him. "Some people think otherwise," he had declared defiantly. But what was eating Janet?

"Which words?" I asked.

"You know which words. Words like 'hell' and 'damn' and 'God.'" It took considerable effort for her to make that speech.

I sputtered, "Well…I don't know. I never noticed…If it offends you, of course…."

Janet finished her degree, taught in the public schools for several years before going back to school for a master's degree, and eventually joined the faculty at the same college where I had been her teacher. I have been told that she is strong, resourceful, demanding, and especially insistent on accurate spelling and grammar in her students' reports.

Under my eyes, Jean was transformed from a high school snowflake queen to a serious and brilliant professional. I was her graduate adviser over this span. We argued about personal values, about the meaning of being Jewish, about Chomsky and behaviorism, about the nature of science and scientific methodology. I came to know her

63

husband well—and to be as fond of him as I was of Jean. He became my handball partner. He was a fabulous athlete who trounced me gently, always teaching me about the game. I watched with pain as they drifted apart, Jean becoming increasingly absorbed in her studies and in the pursuit of recognition as well as excellence. She moved forward in her professional world and also toward an inevitable divorce. When she remarried, it was to another professional who, like her, was immersed in his profession.

I had a chance meeting with her mother. I introduced myself as Jean's former professor and told her how sorry I was that the marriage had failed.

Jean's mother eyed me coldly. "You were her adviser. Maybe if you had advised her that not only her professional work is important, she wouldn't have needed a divorce."

With Gail, another of my students, I must have touched a spiritual note. After she graduated she continued to send an annual Christmas card filled with heartwarming stories of Christian charity, Christian courage, Christian morality, Christian generosity. One year I could endure it no more. I responded and asked whether there were fundamental differences between Christian and Jewish charity, courage, or morality. It took another two years before I was dropped from her Christmas list.

Ann was among my favorite students when I first began teaching in Fargo. She had an open smile, an easy laugh, and intelligence. She would be successful and happy. How could she be otherwise? I had not heard from Ann for fifteen years and was elated when she called me at the University of Minnesota and arranged to visit me. It's always exciting for me to reconnect with someone I taught very early in my career. I try to forbear asking what I was really like, what they thought of me as I taught my first classes. But when I met Ann my excitement evaporated in an instant. Ann of the dancing eyes did not appear. In her place was an emaciated, vacant woman with trembling hands and eyes that registered nothing. Her marriage had broken up. Her husband had the children and she was not allowed to visit them. She was alcoholic and severely ill. She needed a job and wanted me to write a letter of recommendation. I wrote the letter and spoke with her employer, urging him to give her a chance. She was hired, but lasted only a week before she was fired for missing work and being drunk when she showed up. Now she has disappeared again.

I have one memory that's composed of odd parts that don't quite fit together, like pieces from different jigsaw puzzles. In the summer of 1961, just before coming to Minnesota, I was a guest faculty member at the University of Iowa and Bob Hanson had been assigned to assist me in one of my courses. Recently I saw him again at a conference and he recalled an episode.

"Do you remember your other assistant the summer you taught at Iowa?" he asked.

"Not really. My memories about that entire summer are vague, except for my anxiety about teaching in the same program I'd graduated from four years earlier."

"But don't you remember Tom Riegert? I was so impressed. He had suffered a severe hearing loss, but nobody on that faculty had talked with him about the problems he would face if he became a therapist. Even though you were there only for one summer, you spoke openly and directly about what he might encounter."

"I can't recall," I said. "But it's the kind of fool-headed thing I might do."

"It meant a lot to Tom," Bob went on. "He changed the direction of his career and specialized in research, and you know how well he has done."

I knew Riegert had a considerable reputation as a speech scientist, but I had never even faintly imagined it had anything to do with me. What a wonderful revelation. This is the kind of story a teacher cherishes but rarely hears.

All was well until a colleague added another, unwelcome piece to the puzzle. She too asked me whether I recalled Tom Riegert.

"What a coincidence," I said. "I was just talking about him with Bob Hanson. It seems I helped launch him on his career."

"That's interesting," she responded. "I met Tom at the Acoustical Society meetings and he mentioned an incident he'd had with you

65

years ago, when you tried to talk him out of the field. He said you were blunt and tactless, and that he went into research despite you."

I can't choose between these two versions of an episode that happened more than twenty years ago and that I can only dimly remember. I wish I could discipline my memory to make the more noble, buoyant version dominate. Alas, the second version forces its way into my thoughts, for who can discipline such memories? They come or resist at will.

There are other memories, of course. Some of the most troubling go back to the turbulence during the Vietnam War, when I was suddenly the enemy to some of the students for whom I had affection and admiration. Victor, who failed his examinations during that period, is probably still convinced that he fell victim to my weak-kneed liberalism when he was calling for campus radicalism.

Teaching has always involved at least some confrontation. I typically required a term paper for my speech development class. Debbie was furious when I criticized her paper for lacking focus. She took that as an attack against her intelligence, her integrity, and her dedication. Marla found it impossible to remain in my course when she learned that I would be discussing learning theory. Learning theory, she told me, makes her physically ill. The following year, Sandy dropped the course because the idea that children develop speech as they mature conflicted with his Zen belief in the grace and perfection of the infant child. One student whose name I never learned came faithfully to class with her boyfriend and necked with him in the last row. I'm not even sure she was registered for the course.

Mary invited me to sing at her wedding, and Judy to speak at her church. I was to be godfather to Len's son, but he had a girl. Joe was the first of my students to carry a purse. Or was it Don, who later became a priest? Jim was having an awful time with his stuttering during a convention presentation some years after he had graduated and become a professional in his own right. Exasperated, he pointed a finger at me in the audience and blurted out, "I haven't had this much trouble since taking his seminar."

Times change, even in the changeless university. We used to begin class by calling the roll. Now students come and go as they please and sit where they wish. That makes it even harder for me to learn names and faces. I suppose it's fortunate that I'm getting older. People are more forgiving. My age has finally caught up to my affliction. Still, there are some students I will remember for many years while many more have vanished without a trace. I've been collecting names for several decades now. Perhaps it's time for a gold watch. No. It's time for a new roll book. The new names must be entered, grades recorded, memories sequestered.

# Two Out in the Bottom of the Ninth

THE EPISODE HAS BEEN clanging in my memory for several years. We were having a faculty meeting. Senior staff were reviewing the progress and accomplishments of junior faculty. Cindy was one of the people being evaluated. She had been hired two years earlier to replace an audiologist who had not measured up and had been let go. It was time to consider whether Cindy would have a permanent appointment or be given a year to find another job. Her main responsibility was to supervise students who were planning to be audiologists and speech clinicians. She was relatively young, in her mid-thirties, with an MA degree from a good institution and prior experience in the field. She took a personal interest in the students and encouraged them to be open with her. In turn, she shared personal aspects of her own life, her marriages, her relations with her parents, her insecurities. She was devoted, hardworking, and eager, but her personal style confounded some of the faculty and, apparently, some of the students. This was reflected in the student evaluations the chairman had obtained. Some loved her dearly, others found her interest and personal revelations to be unsettling and intrusive.

I was in the waning years of my academic career, one of the older faculty members who had evolved into a guardian of past traditions. The department was moving in other directions, less personal, more businesslike, more concerned with getting large numbers of students in and out. At faculty meetings I had become a voice that spoke in antique accents, seemingly out of touch with current academic realities.

I sat quietly through most of the discussion of Cindy's future with the department. I wasn't sure about her professional competence. Her specialty was quite different than mine. I was quite fond of her, however. I was certain that she cared greatly for the department, for the students, and for the clients they served. She was insecure and pushed a bit too hard, worked too hard at being pleasant and congenial, but she was still young, still learning her role in an academic department with people she held in awe. As I listened to the discussion, I could understand why some aspects of her behavior were being criticized, but I felt that she deserved more time to acclimate.

I was surprised at the seriousness with which the negative remarks from students about her performance were being taken. For every student who had a peeve, another had been very complimentary. She was not nearly as emotionally reserved as some of the faculty who were now judging her, and they clearly considered that a very serious lapse in professionalism. In fact, Cindy had called me the night before the faculty meeting, very distraught, suffering from the thought that her colleagues—her friends—would be judging her and possibly finding fault with her. She had a premonition that they might question her ability. I saw her the next day just before the faculty meeting. She was still very emotional.

The discussion was winding down to a conclusion. It was time for a vote. I hadn't participated much. I was discouraged at the critical tone that was being used to bolster a harsh judgment. The vote was counted. Cindy didn't have enough votes to continue on in her position. We were ordered by the chair not to reveal the discussion or the outcome. We were to conclude our meeting, go out into the corridor, look past Cindy's office where she would be waiting expectantly, and say nothing.

As the faculty were preparing to leave, I asked for a moment's consideration.

"I've been wondering. Have these concerns been brought to Cindy's attention? Has she been given a chance to respond, or to change her approach to the students?"

There was no immediate response. Finally the chair said, "I don't think so."

I continued. "Have we considered the effect this decision might have on the professional community? Cindy is an officer in the state association and very popular with working clinicians. Two such dismissals in so short a time would suggest that we were creating an unreasonable environment for new clinical faculty. There are already mutterings about elite professors holed up in their ivory tower, not mindful of the real problems in the clinical world. I'm concerned that we may be making a rash decision."

There was silence, then further discussion.

A faculty member said, "One of us could serve as Cindy's mentor, to give her some guidance in clinical supervision."

"Yes," said another, "and we can have a review in a year to see whether she's making satisfactory progress."

Still another said, "I'd be glad to be her mentor; I'd enjoy working with her."

The tone of the meeting had changed. There now seemed many possible alternatives to firing Cindy. The chair called for a new vote. It was favorable and Cindy was retained. Once again the chair reminded us not to reveal anything about our deliberations. We filed out and as we passed Cindy, I broke the rules. I gave her a sign indicating all was well.

Shirley stopped me as I was leaving. "We were losing, and it was two out in the bottom of the ninth," she said, "and you hit a home run."

Cindy easily sailed through her next year's probation and remained on the faculty for several more years before deciding to take another position. The departmental party bidding her farewell was filled with well-wishers offering warm appreciation. I pulled Shirley aside and commented on the difference between this event and that earlier faculty meeting.

"Do you remember what you said at the close of that meeting?" I asked. "You used a baseball analogy."

She didn't know what I was referring to. She had completely forgotten.

Several years after I retired from the University I had a call from Cindy telling me that I had been selected to receive a lifetime achievement award from our professional state association. At the awards banquet she introduced me and read the citation she had compiled listing my achievements. There were tears in her eyes as we embraced on the podium. In mine, too.

# Turtle Mania

TURTLES LIVE IN EVERY nook and cranny of my house—on shelves, in bookcases, on the mantle over the fireplace, in a special cabinet with glass doors that's filled to overcrawling, in the cubbies of my rolltop desk. I have close to two hundred at last count, from all over the world, made of glass, pewter, crystal, clay, wood, dried seeds, silver, porcelain, plastic, nuts and bolts, pebbles, cardboard. Most can fit in the palm of my hand, but one is large enough to use as a doorstop and some are vanishingly tiny. All are decorative; some are also functional. I have one with holes in the top that I assumed was a pencil caddy until, after several years, I had an uncontrollable urge to blow into it and discovered it's a kind of flute. Others have secret compartments. My granddaughter Elana is especially fond of a silver turtle that's a music box. The green plastic turtle that undulated suggestively across the floor when it was wound up has long since expired.

At first I kept a record of who gave me each turtle, but that eventually proved too burdensome. Now most of them are of uncertain origin. Although I have a large collection, I didn't buy any of them. They were all given to me as gifts. It started in 1978, when I began a five-year term as director of the Cognitive Sciences Center at the University of Minnesota. The center is an interdisciplinary research and training consortium made up of a select group of faculty and advanced graduate students from various departments of the University.

The first director of the center was Professor Jim Jenkins, an experimental psychologist. At the beginning of each year, when the new students arrived, Jenkins would greet them with the same apocryphal story:

It seems that the great psychologist and philosopher William James was giving a public lecture. During the lecture he commented dramatically that even though we live in the midst of a sea of other planets, in unbounded space, no one knows for certain how the earth remains suspended in the solar system, and why it doesn't fall from the skies and plunge us all into eternal oblivion

When the lecture had ended, an elderly woman accosted the great psychologist and said that she knew why the earth remains suspended in space. "It's because the world is resting snugly on the back of a gigantic turtle."

The professor, who was still basking in the enthusiasm his lecture had provoked, smiled benevolently and said, "That's all very well, madam, but then we are faced with the dilemma of what is holding up the turtle."

"Oh," she said. "It's another turtle."

The professor was becoming a bit irritated by the woman's insistence, but still he responded charitably: "That will get us nowhere, my good woman, because we must then ask what the second turtle is resting on, ad infinitum."

She responded without hesitation, "You don't understand, Professor. It's turtles, all the way down to the bottom."

From the first telling of that anecdote, turtles became the official logo and mascot of the center, and T-shirts with turtles piled one on top of another (or in other configurations) were printed up and proudly worn by the members. When I became director of the center, my wife marked the occasion by giving me a pewter turtle. I was touched but had no notion at the time how rapidly turtles can multiply. From then on I was flooded with turtles, from my wife on every major occasion, from my children on those occasions they remembered, from my students as they returned from the exotic places they had visited over spring break or as they gratefully took leave of the university, from a janitor in my building who, seeing my growing collection, decided to feed this obsession, from children who passed my office on the way to the speech clinic and there crafted turtles of wood or paper or paper clips, and from strangers who never identified themselves but mysteriously left turtles on my desk.

I long ago lost control of the turtle population. I have announced to family members that the time has come to think more carefully about what to buy me on birthdays or Father's Day. I have called various local stores and warned them that my wife suffers from "turtle mania," and that they could be perpetuating a deep-seated disturbance by encouraging or even allowing her to buy a turtle should she appear in their shop. I have pushed my wife out of gift shops just as she was reaching for another magnificent example of the myriad ways a turtle can be rendered, only to discover that she later sneaked back and had a surprise for me when we returned home. I have spoken as forcefully on the subject as good manners and decorum would allow, but still the turtles have been fruitful and multiplied.

It is not quite accurate to suggest that these mute replicas are the first turtles to have been introduced into my life. When my children were young we had the usual experience with painted turtles in fish tanks that too soon became their burial grounds. None lasted more than a few days, probably because we couldn't curb the solicitous concern of our three small children.

There is another turtle tale that has gone into the folklore of our family. Many years ago, when my mother came to visit us from New York, we all went for an outing to the Como Zoo in St. Paul. After walking in and out of numerous exhibitions, my weary mother sat down for a moment on one of two large carved turtles that had been placed invitingly at the entrance to the cat house. Suddenly the statue heaved itself up and lumbered a few steps forward before again freezing into immobility. The turtles were ancient, huge—and alive! If turtles can hear, that poor creature and its mate suffered a permanent hearing loss from the shrieks of terror from my mother, and of glee from my children.

For many years I kept most of my turtle collection in a cabinet at my university office. Occasionally students from distant lands would notice the collection and would comment on the symbolism of turtles in their native countries. It was an occasion for cultural edification.

In many places, it was traditionally believed that the world sits on the back of a gigantic turtle, as in the James story; turtles are also indicators of long life, wisdom, or fertility. In the spring of 1997, when I retired from the university after thirty-six years on the faculty, colleagues presented me with a gift in a large, heavy box. I opened it with a frozen smile on my face, fearing it would be the mother of all turtles, the one the university, if not the universe, rests on. I was thoroughly relieved to find it was instead a beautiful vase created by the world-class potter Warren MacKenzie, who was also retired from the University of Minnesota.

A lovely gift. But when I got home I found that the place where I intended to display my new pottery was already occupied by a piece of furniture. My ever thoughtful wife had arranged to obtain the old cabinet from my university office that had housed all my turtles. Now I could display them at home. And the truly good news, my wife informed me, was that I would also have room for the new turtles I would undoubtedly want to collect, especially now that I had so much time to search for the little treasures.

# The Quality of Mercy

OUR FIRST TWO CHILDREN were born in a Catholic hospital in Prescott, Kansas, much to the astonishment of our families back in Brooklyn. There were perhaps a half a dozen Jews in Prescott when we arrived in 1959. We added significantly to those numbers with the birth of David and Karen. David was reputedly the first Jewish boy ever born in the town. Karen's birth, fourteen months later, should have been less remarkable except for a non-medical complication that developed just as Eileen's delivery date was approaching.

When Eileen was into her third month of pregnancy, the county commissioners voted to raze the old St. Joseph's Hospital where David had been born and build a new one in its place. That should have been welcome news: a brand-new, up-to-date, modern facility for our second child. But there was a hitch. The city fathers and mothers decided that the Catholic nuns, who had staffed and managed the old hospital for many decades, were no longer needed—or welcome. With hardly a proper thank-you, the Sisters of Mercy were informed that they would have no place in the new facility. The Sisters protested that they were fully capable of functioning in a new hospital and had been looking forward to the opportunity during the many years they had struggled to provide quality care despite the limitations of old St. Joseph's. Their arguments fell on deaf ears. They had to move on. Progress had to be served.

The Sisters resolved to leave in a way that would teach the community a lesson in fair-mindedness. They announced that they would abandon the old hospital in January, when their contract expired, rather than continue on until June when the new facility would be completed and the new staff would be hired.

The Sisters had been wonderful to us during David's birth and I felt they were being badly treated. I congratulated them on their courage and determination—but mostly I panicked. Our baby was due in February during that interval when the hospital would have to close because there would be no nurses or attendants to staff it. Neither Eileen nor I had any romantic desire to bring our child into the world in our living room.

I found several other families in Prescott who were expecting and were similarly concerned about having to travel many miles to deliver. We gathered at our home one night and formulated a petition, pleading with the Sisters to set aside their righteous indignation and to stay on until the new facility was up and running. We then hit the streets to garner support. I signed my name at the top of one petition and began knocking on doors, hoping to touch the hearts and conscience of our neighbors.

I soon discovered that the sight of someone at the door with a clipboard was signal enough to many of the householders that there was important work to be done in the cellar, the attic, or a remote part of their backyard. Occasionally I succeeded in getting the front door to open at least a crack, at which point I hurriedly launched my prepared spiel:

"Pardon me, madam, but you know the Sisters have announced they will quit St. Joseph's before the new hospital is completed, and that means we won't have a hospital for several months, and my wife is going to deliver a baby during those months, so we are trying to persuade the Sisters to stay, and we've got a petition here asking them to reconsider."

Had I been a sociologist or ethnographer, rather than a worried parent, I might have found the experience enlightening. I've recorded some of my neighbors' reactions.

Neighbor 1: "Didn't you ever learn about birth control?"

Me: "Yes, ma'am, we do know about the birds and the bees, but we didn't know St. Joseph's was going to close."

Neighbor 2: "We don't have money to squander on frivolous causes."

Me: "But ma'am, we are not asking you to dip into your life savings. We only want your signature on this petition to the Sisters."

Neighbor 3: "Is this one of those Communist things?"

Me: "I understand your concerns, sir, but I can guarantee this has absolutely nothing to do with either the Communist or the Democratic Party."

Neighbor 4: "I don't like to sign petitions, but…"

Me: "I agree that one can't be too careful these days, but I do think you should sign your own name, and not your sister's who lives in Tulsa."

Neighbor 5: "Is the Pope involved in this? I don't much care for the Pope."

Me: "This petition has nothing to do with the Pope. I'm Jewish myself. Yes sir, Jewish, but I'm getting along fine, thank you, except for this hospital business."

Neighbor 6: "That's awful, young man. We'll pray for you."

Me: "That's really kind of you, and I'm sure your prayers will help, but won't you sign the petition too?"

So it went for several weeks. Of course, many people were sympathetic and willingly signed our petition. When we pooled our work, we had quite a few names but not nearly as many as I had hoped for. I began to make plans to fly Eileen to New York so the baby could be born in a hospital.

In the end my fears were unwarranted. Even before I could deliver our signed petitions, the Sisters announced they would stay on. I suspect they had intended to from the start.

Karen was born in St. Joseph's Hospital on February 3, 1961, totally oblivious to the drama playing out around her. Soon afterwards St. Joseph's closed its doors for good. I'm not certain whether David was truly the first Jewish boy born in Prescott, but Karen was surely the last Jewish girl to be swaddled and embraced by the nuns at St. Joseph's.

Some years later, when the children were in their early teens, we returned to Prescott for a summer and I saw the elegant new county hospital. It was quite imposing. I am glad, however, that our children breathed their first in the old St. Joseph's. I sometimes think that Karen, especially, owed her gentle nature in part to the loving care of those gracious Sisters who ultimately demonstrated, to my great relief and gratitude, that the quality of mercy cannot be strained.

# Richard Dyer-Bennet

## 1. A Story

THE DAY BEGAN COLD and blustery. Then the snow started falling—the beginning of another North Dakota blizzard. Richard Dyer-Bennet, singer of folk songs, classical guitarist, and minstrel, was to perform that evening at Concordia College. The concert had been scheduled for the college's field house, in anticipation of a large audience, but because of the storm and an outbreak of influenza on campus, there were no more than two or three dozen people in the audience. The auditorium looked empty and cavernous.

The concert began exactly on time. Mr. Dyer-Bennet, precise and professional, was dressed in a tuxedo, and not noticeably affected by the small audience. He sang a great variety of songs in his high tenor—songs from America, Ireland, England, and Scotland, ballads, work songs, spirituals, and sea shanties, accompanying himself on the guitar and making each song inimitably his own. He brought drama to the storytelling, playfully hinting at double entendres and effortlessly calling up the emotions latent in each of the pieces. He addressed the audience directly only once, explaining that to portray the mood of a particular song it would be necessary for him to turn his back for a moment. He asked the audience's indulgence. At no point were listeners invited to sing along or clap their hands or join in the chorus. Dyer-Bennet was giving a classical concert, not leading a hootenanny.

He ended the performance with a haunting rendition of the spiritual "Lonesome Valley." On this last piece, rather than plucking or strumming the strings of his guitar, Dyer-Bennet gently hammered them in a syncopated rhythm of increasing intensity as his high tenor voice soared above the airy sound. He took his final bows and the audience, reluctantly, began to make their way to the exits.

One woman—middle-aged, intense, uncomfortable—remained behind. Hesitantly, she approached the stage. She was frail and tentative, but her voice was surprisingly strong.

"You sang beautifully, Mr. Dyer-Bennet. It was a wonderful concert, but that last song, 'Lonesome Valley,' that song is wrong."

"I'm sorry you didn't enjoy it," he responded.

She shook her head. "It's not a matter of enjoyment, Mr. Dyer-Bennet. It's a matter of salvation."

"I don't understand."

"The words you sang, they say you've got to cross the valley, the Lonesome Valley, by yourself."

"Yes. Those are the words to the song."

"But they are all wrong. We have to cross the valley with our Savior, with Jesus, not by ourselves."

Dyer-Bennet paused, weighing his answer. "That may be your personal belief, but it's not what the song intends. That's not how I understand the song, and so I wouldn't be artistically honest were I to present it as you suggest."

The woman was excited now. "Artistic honesty is nothing compared to God's eternal truth. Everything in our lives, even our songs, have to be in harmony with God's truth, and Jesus has taught us to take life's journey in his protecting embrace."

"That may be true for you," he answered softly, "but we must each find our own path to spirituality. You find it in Christianity, I in my music, and so I must perform the songs faithfully as I understand them."

A bleak grayness descended on the woman. Grimly, with no further comment, she turned and shuffled down the aisle toward the exit doors. She was quite lame and dragged one foot as she retreated. Her posture, her gait were like a judgment. Before she reached the door she turned. Her voice quivered with intensity. "I will pray for you, Mr. Dyer-Bennet. I will pray for your immortal soul."

She turned again and walked more vigorously now, her lame foot dragging, until she finally vanished. Dyer-Bennet looked thoughtfully after her. Then he packed up his music and his instrument, and went out into the cold night. The storm had abated, the air was incredibly clear and cold, and the sky was filled with brilliant stars. It was a frozen but beautiful night.

A car pulled up and Dyer-Bennet climbed in, carefully setting his guitar on the seat beside him. Tomorrow he was to give a series of master classes for students in the music program, followed by another concert in the same hall that evening. If the snow held off, the audience would surely be larger.

The car windows were frosted over and he could see very little as he crossed the bridge to his hotel in Fargo. Softly, meditatively, without realizing it, he began to sing the words of the old spiritual to himself:

*You've got to cross that Lonesome Valley.*
*You've got to cross it by yourself.*
*There ain't no one there to cross it for you.*
*You've got to cross it by yourself.*

## 2. A Memoir

I became enthralled with Richard Dyer-Bennet as a teenager, soon after I discovered the redemptive quality of folk music, in the late 1940s. At college I was drawn to any circle that included a folksinger. I participated in the endless debates about the authenticity of various singers and their renditions of songs: Dyer-Bennet, Burl Ives, John Jacob Niles, Pete Seeger, Josh White, Leadbelly. When I married, our closest friends gave us a sampling of folk records as a wedding gift, including one disk by Dyer-Bennet. It took me some time to appreciate his voice, almost a countertenor, and his dramatic presentation. He was a trained musician, not a rustic, untutored singer who had been discovered by an ethnomusicologist or simply wandered into the recording studio from the hill country or a chain gang. Neither was he a pampered New Yorker who fervently wished he'd been born in the mountains of West Virginia or the Delta cotton-fields. He considered himself a minstrel, and not a folksinger at all.

My wife and I were among the few who braved the elements to hear Dyer-Bennet perform on that wintery night in 1958. At the time I was on the faculty of North Dakota Agricultural College in Fargo, just across the river from Concordia College. At the end of the first night's concert we sat, riveted, in our seats as the small audience filed out. No one showed up to drive Dyer-Bennet to his hotel; apparently there had been a mix-up, and he was stranded. Timidly, I volunteered. Into our 1948 Studebaker we squeezed him, his guitar, two friends who had come with us, and Archie Lieberman, a photographer who was accompanying Dyer-Bennet on tour to take pictures for a story to appear in *Coronet Magazine*. Dyer-Bennet invited us to join him for coffee and so I had the enormous pleasure of informal conversation with him. My wife and I, of course, were back in our seats the next night for the second concert, and again we provided his transportation and joined him for coffee after the concert.

During the course of these conversations, which seemed almost magical to me, Dyer-Bennet acknowledged that his children preferred Burl Ives to him, but was confident their opinions would change as they matured. He was being neither arrogant nor condescending. Rather, he was expressing a sure judgment of his own ability and talent. He felt that Josh White was a fine performer who had been badly advised that formal musical training would interfere with his natural gifts. It is always best, he said, to strive consciously to improve one's talents and skills. Though we were discussing music, Dyer-Bennet seemed to be commenting on all aspects of life: the need to maintain integrity, to strive for improvement in any undertaking.

He mentioned that he was starting his own recording label so that he would have greater artistic control of his recordings. I bought the records he produced under his own label and wore them out.

The explosion of interest in folk music eventually waned. In the late 1950s and '60s folk music blended with popular music. Burl Ives recorded "A Little Bit of Tear Let Me Down," and a new breed of performer, exemplified by The Kingston Trio and Peter, Paul and Mary, brought many of the songs I loved to a wider audience, but in arrangements that seemed slick and contrived. Folksingers became comedians who parodied the music, or activists who exploited it. There no longer was a commitment to render to the song what it was due.

Dyer-Bennet's recordings eventually disappeared from the catalogs and the music stores. In my home there is a private joke for which the punch line is, "Would anyone like to hear Richard Dyer-Bennet?" When my daughter brought home a serious suitor, I put him to the test. He had never heard Dyer-Bennet sing "Lonesome Valley." But, other than my own children, neither has hardly any other person of that generation. I shouldn't be surprised. Not long ago I told a psychology PhD candidate that I had just heard a wonderful recording by Caruso.

"Caruso," he said. "Is that a group?"

It amazes me that although music is so much a part of the lives of young people nowadays, they haven't discovered Dyer-Bennet's artistry and the beauty of his songs. I've become a bore on the subject.

Some twenty-five years after those concerts in Moorhead, I met Dyer-Bennet again. I was on the faculty at the University of Minnesota, living in Minneapolis, and I heard on the radio that he was scheduled to give a series of dramatic readings of the Iliad during the day and a concert of Schubert songs later in the evening. I made my way down to Carleton College where he was to perform, an hour's drive south of Minneapolis, but the concert was a disappointment. It was not the music I wanted to hear, and Dyer-Bennet's voice sounded strained and pinched. I kept hoping he would bring out his guitar and play the songs I loved, but there was no guitar in sight.

At the reception following the concert, I introduced myself. He vaguely recalled having given a performance in Moorhead many years earlier on a frozen night, but little more. He no longer recorded folk music. He had a new project. The Library of Congress had awarded him a grant to record the works of Homer. He was doing extensive research and was undertaking much of the translation himself.

I pressed him about his earlier career, about the possibility he would again perform folk music, but he was interested only discussing his current project. Richard Dyer-Bennet was no longer a minstrel. He had become a Homeric scholar, bringing to that new pursuit the same care, thoughtfulness, absorption, and integrity that had distinguished his musical career.

Richard Dyer-Bennet will always be associated in my mind with stirring renditions of beautiful folk songs and ballads. The Smithsonian Institute has acquired and is distributing all of the recordings he made on his own label and I have been accumulating them again on compact disks. It's odd. I have him frozen in time, but he was quite willing to move on to new artistic challenges. Still, when I listen to him sing "Lonesome Valley," I want to reassure him that he is not alone. I sing along.

# A Grand Idea

LAST NOVEMBER, MY WIFE, Eileen, announced that she would like to take a vacation.

"What a grand idea," I enthused. "Let's find a warm place for a couple of weeks and take some bite out of winter."

But Eileen wasn't thinking of Tucson, Palm Springs, or any of the other spots our friends flee to when Minnesota's harsh winter approaches. She was musing about a different kind of vacation, one that I'm on all the time but never notice.

"What I really want," she said, "is a vacation from my diabetes."

Diabetes has become so much a part of our lives that I'm hardly aware of it. Eileen's wistful remark brought it sharply into the foreground. It reminded me that every day she must draw blood three or four times and inject herself with insulin to maintain good control and avoid the threat of complications.

Eileen's diabetes is a stern teacher, an old-fashioned taskmaster who is quite willing to rap the knuckles of an inattentive student. And school is always in session.

But there was no time for fantasizing about a vacation. Our grandchildren were waiting. We had promised to take them to the Bell Museum of Natural History on the University of Minnesota campus.

We didn't get very far into the exhibits before a woman stopped us.

"How nice to see you again," she said. She seemed genuinely pleased.

"You look familiar," I said, "but I can't quite…"

"Oh, it's been several years, and you were both too upset to remember me, but I haven't forgotten you," she said. She turned to my wife.

"I brought you to your hospital room, just before you were going to celebrate some special occasion—a birthday or an anniversary?"

Of course! It was five years ago. Our daughter, Karen, had come to Minneapolis to help celebrate my sixtieth birthday. She and Eileen were doing some last-minute shopping when Eileen noticed her vision was blurry. She was also extremely thirsty and was constantly running to the bathroom. Karen prevailed on her to see a doctor. The examination was scarcely over before Eileen was admitted to the hospital, her blood sugar over 1,000 mg/dl.

A nurse helped Eileen into a wheelchair and propelled her from the urgent care clinic to Fairview Hospital. I stumbled along behind, shocked and distraught to the point of tears. Eileen wouldn't be able to participate in the big birthday party she had planned—I couldn't imagine celebrating the event without her. And the next week would be our fortieth anniversary. The nurse, kind and solicitous, tried to comfort me. "She'll be fine," she said. "We'll take good care of her for you."

Standing in the natural history museum, that same nurse smiled warmly.

"You two were so sad. My heart went out to you. But you look so much better now, both of you."

"Thank you. Thank you so much!" was all we could manage as our grandson dragged us off to see an "awesome" exhibit of a wolf stalking a gigantic moose.

How touching that the nurse remembered us years later. Indeed, everything is looking better than it did that awful afternoon at the hospital. Eileen still works as a teacher, chasing after four- and five-year-olds in Temple Israel Nursery School. And, of course, there are the visits with our four grandchildren. She continues to be the heart of our family celebrations. Last spring she prepared a traditional feast for the twenty guests who joined us for the first seder of Passover.

Perhaps next winter Eileen and I will take a cruise or follow our friends to some warm and sunny destination. It won't be a vacation from diabetes, but we'll be together, and there is plenty of room in our suitcase for an insulin pen and glucose meter, right next to the garish shorts and outrageous floral shirts.

# Handball Stories

# Handball Fantasy

I'VE PLAYED HANDBALL WITH Morrie Miller practically every week for the last five years. In all of those hundreds of games I have never won. Not even a single game. Once I came close. I was ahead with eighteen points to his fifteen and I was serving. The sun was streaming through a small window near the ceiling of the court in the Cooke Hall tower, and cast a bright square of light in the left corner, near the back wall. Morrie looked up towards the window and squinted, then looked back at the square of light and squinted again, his face contorted as though in pain. I resolved not to cheapen my victory by exploiting a square of light. I served the ball away from the light, to Morrie's strong hand. He flattened the ball and then placed three perfect serves on the bull's-eye, smack in the middle of that square of light. Then, when I was demoralized and confused, he finished me off on the other side. That is as close as I have ever come to beating Morrie Miller.

But I don't despair. One of these days I'll humble him. I'll execute dazzling shots with both hands, placing the ball in corners of the handball court so remote that even Morrie can't reach them. What an occasion that will be: a band will suddenly appear and strike up a triumphant tune. The court will fill far beyond its capacity with cheering spectators; famous personages will come to pay me tribute.

The President will be there, surrounded by Secret Service men. He'll make an impromptu speech to the waiting cameras: "In this great country of ours, all things are possible for those who are willing to dream, to sacrifice, and to strive. These are the qualities that have made America a jewel in the crown of nations. Take note, you weak and downtrodden masses. Persist in your struggle. Remember Jerry

Siegel, a simple and ordinary citizen, who on this day has reached the heights of defeating Morrie Miller."

His words will be greeted by misty eyes and a great cheer. Then there will be a sudden hush. All eyes will turn to the entrance of the court as a succession of handball greats will file in to extend their personal congratulations to a man who has finally beaten Morrie Miller. The crowd, overcome with emotion, will no longer be able to contain itself. A mighty shout will arise:" Hurray! Bravo! Right on! *Mazel tov!*"

Solemnly I will raise my hand to still the cheering throng. "Friends," I will say, "you know I am not one for words. I did my talking on the court, with my swollen and bruised hands. I just want you all to know that this is a victory not just for me. It is for all of us ordinary people who are not inordinately gifted, who are not ambidextrous, who do not have eyes in the back of our heads. This is a victory for the scrappers, who persist with hope and dogged determination."

That great day will come, and I will cherish it. The world will be a better place when I finally triumph over Morrie Miller in a game of handball. I will have given hope to the multitudes by my example. That will be my legacy. Perhaps not this Wednesday, Morrie Miller, but that day will come. It will surely come.

And it will feel very good to win.

# Minutes of the Meeting

THE COOKE HALL HANDBALL CLUB held its annual meeting and banquet at the home of Vice President Anders. The meeting was called to order at 3:30 P.M. As is the custom, wives and significant others were also in attendance.

Club president Adelman called the meeting to order, after which Siegel read the treasurer's report: "Since we don't have any dues or fees, the only money we collect is loose change that falls out of the members' pockets. So far I've collected $11.75, all in front of Pick's locker."

After considerable discussion, it was decided to give the money as a gift of appreciation to Anders, since he was the only player that every other club member could count on beating at least some of the time, and it was important to keep him in the club. Everyone agreed and Balkcum chipped in an additional five dollars of his own money—or so he claimed. He was standing next to Pick at the time.

President Adelman asked if there was any old business and Anders began complaining about various old injuries he'd sustained on the court. Adelman then exposed a scar on his arm from a recent operation following a handball injury. Pick held up several crooked fingers on each hand; Balkcum groaned aloud thinking about all the people he'd struck with the ball during the past year; and Kyle picked up some spare change that fell out of Pick's pocket.

Moving on to current business, Kearney observed that something ought to be done about the condition of the courts in Cooke Hall: no ceilings, poor lighting, bad ventilation, loose boards, uneven court size. Kyle opined that that was old business since the courts were lousy last year too. Kearney said he was so disgusted with the courts he planned to withhold his activity fee next year. Adelman reminded him that he hadn't paid an activity fee for ten years and had been sneaking in and using other people's lockers since he joined the club. Adelman said they'd have to live with the conditions in Cooke Hall because they were all too cheap to go to a fancy club. Passed unanimously.

Siegel proposed that on courts where the windows didn't open, players should be required to change their gym clothes at least twice a year, but the members felt it would be an assault on individual freedom and against the spirit of handball. Wives and significant others had to be reminded at this point that they couldn't vote, and ought to consider themselves privileged even to be listening in to the meeting.

There was another call for new business and Dodds, who had just enrolled in law school, rose to a point of order: "I would like to order two hamburgers with everything, and a double-thick chocolate milk shake." President Adelman reminded Dodds that the banquet would commence when the business meeting finished.

Pick addressed the chair. "Mr. President, I would like to nominate a new member to our club. His name is Yanz. He's young, strong, athletic, and even Anders can beat him." Anders seconded and Yanz was initiated into the club without a dissenting vote. As a sign of acceptance and good will, Yanz was invited to host the next handball banquet. Mrs. Yanz had to be reminded again that women were only observers during the business meeting.

Adelman then called the meeting adjourned, but Dodds objected that the awards had not yet been given. Adelman said the awards were part of the banquet and not the business meeting. Mrs. Adelman said it didn't matter because the meeting had taken so long everything was overcooked anyway. Mrs. Anders said there was still plenty of good, nutritious food for everybody if they would just stop squabbling and finish the meeting. At that, the meeting was shouted to a close, the club members changed out of their handball uniforms into street clothes—except for Adelman, who doesn't own street clothes. The meeting was officially adjourned and the banquet began at 7:32 P.M.

At the awards dinner, the following members were honored:

Most improved player—new member Yanz.

Sportsmanship award—Dodds, for helping Feinberg to his feet after tripping him on the court.

Best record—Siegel, for coming late to thirty-six consecutive matches.

Best defensive maneuvers—Balkcum, for his consistency in calling hinders on tough shots that he couldn't reach.

Best passing shot—Kyle, who has a digestive problem.

Finally, a special Commendation for Courage was awarded to the president's wife, Bobby Adelman, who has survived all these years in the same bed with a husband who replays all of his matches in the evening, in bed, after he falls asleep.

Respectfully submitted, Jerry Siegel, Secretary and Treasurer.

# The Cooke Hall Consortium

THEY CAME FROM ALL OVER the Twin Cities, and even from abroad. They came on foot, bike, and poodle-drawn Datsun. By ones and twos they filed into an ordinary looking home on a corner of an ordinary neighborhood in South Minneapolis. They ranged in age from the 30s to the 60s. To the casual observer, there was nothing special about them. They might have been a church group attending a Sunday afternoon Bible study; or, from the pans of food they brought along, a gourmet club. The women were handsome and regal. They helped their husbands climb the stairs and then guided the men to the more comfortable chairs in the crowded living room.

On closer inspection, there was something arresting about these men. One sensed their unusually low blood pressure and their slowed heart rate. One could tell they were accustomed to combat. As they entered the house, leaning heavily on the arms of their wives, one could see the steely glint, the unwavering resolve of persons who were used to making split-second decisions and who knew how to cut their losses when necessary. They were warriors, gladiators. With no weapons other than their wits and their hands, they challenged each other in jousts of skill, strength, and endurance in the archaic, crumbling ruins of Cooke Hall gymnasium. They were twice- or thrice-weekly combatants in the great game of handball. Let us meet them individually.

First, meet "Ageless Adelman," still competing into his seventh decade. On the exterior a gentle man, a lover of opera, soft-spoken, quiet, unfailingly polite—but inside, a man of iron and steel. He is a relentless foe on the court who never concedes defeat. Armed with years of combat experience in the Air Force (and his first marriage), Adelman will resort to any ruse to win. In a tense moment in a match with Karni, he cruelly launched into the love duet from the Magic Flute, singing both the Papageno and Papagena parts until Karni fled the court.

"Zahareas" is a name that conjures images of ancient Greek history, dangerous voyages and adventures. As the game proceeds, he attacks his opponent with an unbroken string of commentaries, analyses, sage comments, compliments on his opponent's style of play. He uses his verbosity like a mighty sword, breaking his opponent's concentration, then his resolve.

"Peerless Pick" plunges after the ball while flinging his opponent out of the way. He crashes into walls and his partners with equal disdain, stopping only to rattle off twenty-seven pushups between serves. Heedless of pain, unaffected by ordinary sensations, this handball machine with the bionic nose plays game after game wearing the same unwashed gym clothes that he wore during his final exam as a doctoral student at Cornell University. He alone is responsible for the rotting floors in those ancient dungeons that form the handball coliseum.

"Elegant Elvin" Balkcum has dedicated his life to handball. His training program includes countless hours on Nautilus machines practicing his special brand of miserable, heart-wrenching moans. Deception is his game, with a first name that has an "E" where an "A" ought to be and his last name a "C" where nothing ought to be. His opponents become distracted, bewildered, and finally confused by his carefully coordinated handball attire and his sleek movements on the court.

There is no corner of the court that "Ralph the Retriever" doesn't know intimately. His pleasure is flinging himself after an errant ball, catapulting himself across the court using a loose floorboard as a spring. Doing the impossible is his game. Ordinary points do not count, only the number of impossible shots he has returned. He last won a game years ago, but he continues doggedly in his search for the perfect retrieve. He has never been heard to complain, cry foul, or curse his fate. Nonetheless, he is allowed to play, another example of the generosity of the handball fraternity.

There was a time when "Tom the Terrible," a professor of English, occupied himself with arcane documents and classic literature. No more. Handball is now his only poetry. All else is pallid prose, purposeless and prosaic. To kill or not to kill, that is the question. Whether 'tis better to suffer the ball to pass you by and to wait for the back-wall shot, or, seizing the moment, to pluck the missile out of the air, and thence to drive it fiercely, forcefully, flawlessly to the front wall—or into your opponent's back.

"Youthful Yanz" is a mere lad who had to grow a beard to gain entry to the gym. He is at the peak of his physical prowess and will eventually catch up in handball prowess. He hits with power and a lack of accuracy that strikes terror in his opponents. He chases every ball, fleetly darting all over the court. He is more energized at the end of a match than at the start. He is the future. As age, worry, and marriage toughen his mind and body, he will become a champion. In the meantime, the elders feast on his inexperience.

"Carnivorous Karni" is all touch, smooth and silky as he slithers toward the ball, never hurrying, but devouring everything in his way. On a good day he spits out handballs like sunflower husks. A native of Northern Minnesota, Karni has never lost the sophisticated style of his Finnish ancestors. Master of the "psych," he plays on the nerves of his opponents, leaving them quivering and anxious, and an easy prey for his overhand pass.

"David the Invincible" is by profession an artist, a painter. In handball he is also an artist with pristine control of the flight of the ball and an endless assortment of shots that he executes equally with both hands. He has yet to be bested by any in this crowd. David is the player the rest of us dream of beating, when the body is at tune with the soul, when the spirit and the flesh become one, when all our shots are miraculously accurate. On that day we will all merge into a giant canvass of handball players, all champions, all unbeatable, all beating each other in the ultimate paradox that is realized in the unreachable handball dream.

# He Might Have Been Champ

FOR ME, HANDBALL ISN'T just another game. It's a family heritage, passed on from my uncles Abe and Meyer. I started playing handball against the wall of Izzy's candy store with one of the pink, high-bouncing "spaldeens" that we used for all of our street games. I'm convinced that the first true environmentalists were the street kids who grew up in Brooklyn in the 1930s and '40s. We used every surface and space the environment provided for some kind of street game—we wasted nothing. Old tennis balls were stripped of their outer shells and used for handball. Rubber bands were hoarded to make new balls. Wooden crates were converted to scooters. Chewing gum was placed on the end of sticks to probe the dark interior of sewers to see what would adhere. These were the raw materials that we lovingly recycled. What a tragedy when one of our precious spaldeens rolled into a sewer. What joy when one was retrieved by a stick and chewing gum.

Those of us destined for real handball soon outgrew Izzy's wall and moved to the school yards and parks to play against a single concrete wall, dodging baseballs and basketballs rather than Izzy. I don't remember when I first hit a real handball, but I know we had no gloves and simply toughed it out until the pain and swelling abated. I'm not sure why I stuck it out, except that there was always something magical about that fiercely competitive game that no other sport could approximate. Putting aside my childish ways, I forsook stickball, punchball, basketball. It had to be handball.

The game had another attraction. My uncles Abe and Meyer played four-wall, on real courts, with ceilings and wooden floors, lights, a gallery, and gloves that matched. I watched them compete at

Raven Hall in Coney Island or the Brooklyn YMCA and they filled me with stories of the great players they had seen and competed against. Abe had been in the navy and had played handball all over the world, challenging local champions at every port, invited into the homes of strangers because he was part of the handball fraternity. Sometimes Abe and Meyer teamed up in doubles. Both were left-handed, but they had different styles and temperaments. Meyer was quick, wiry, and deceptively strong. Abe was more deliberate. His serve did a 45° when it hit the floor and he had a vicious kill from the back wall. Abe played patient control. Meyer was always on the attack. There were other differences. Abe was younger and unmarried. Meyer raced to the courts from his grocery store and then raced out to the market and then back to his family. Meyer squeezed handball into his life. Abe made handball integral in his.

Meyer credits me ignobly with taking him off the courts for good. I was back from the University of Iowa one summer. In Iowa I had finally taken up the game seriously, and I came back to New York brimming with enthusiasm. Meyer decided it was finally time to give his young nephew a lesson, and he brought me to Raven Hall to demonstrate some of the nuances of the game.

He started with the service. He lined me up in the back court, lofted the ball gracefully into the deep left corner, and grunted with pain. Something went out in his shoulder and he hasn't had full motion since. I stood in the back court, excited and nervous, savoring the anticipation of playing handball with one of my boyhood heroes, but the game was over and I never touched the ball. Meyer has retold the story many times. Each time the contest gets longer, the game more thrilling, and the outcome more uncertain. But he always suffers his injury just as he was finally about to put the game away.

I eventually got onto the court with Abe, too. Abe played the kind of smart game that could go on forever, and he kept improving at it. He and "Coop," his lifelong handball partner, played in the masters and got a write-up in *Handball Magazine* after the St. Louis Nationals. It looked good for Abe. He was a young fifty and ready to challenge the old-timers. If that didn't pan out, there was the super-masters. He

## HE MIGHT HAVE BEEN CHAMP

had a bright future and he might have been champ, but he got cut down in an unexpected way, though not until he gave me the lesson that Uncle Meyer had intended.

When he was fifty-five years old, Abe drove all the way to Minnesota, into the wilds of the Midwest, to the tiny village of Minneapolis. No other family member had dared venture so far west, but Abe was a man of courage, having survived World War II, the Lower East Side, and uncounted hero sandwiches from Meyer's grocery store. He stayed with us for a week, though it was only a few days before he was to return that he quietly mentioned that he had brought along his gym equipment.

The match was set up for the next evening at Cooke Hall, an aboveground dungeon where University of Minnesota faculty and students played handball and racquetball on courts that were all different sizes—none of them regulation—with sloping floors, no ceilings, and bad lighting. In these familiar environs, I thought, I might have a chance against the newcomer, who would be robbed of the ceiling game I had never developed, and who didn't know the soft spots in the walls and floors. Abe's uniform consisted of a pair of faded shorts, a tattered sweatshirt with the sleeves torn off, and a pair of work gloves.

"Do you need some gloves?" I asked.

"Nah. These are what I always use. What about the ceiling?"

"Out," I said. He looked at the court and shook his head with sympathy.

After a few casual tosses, he asked me to serve. I gave him my patented left side serve, and he promptly killed it. "Dummy, he's a lefty," I reminded myself.

His first serve came to my power, and then veered sharply. I flailed at the ball. My face reddened. The second serve did the same, but not so sharply. I fanned again. The next couple of serves broke the other way, catching me leaning awkwardly. It started to look like a quick game and a long evening when, mercifully, he stopped putting a spin on the ball and I could volley. It turned into a close game, and I won.

The second game was all Abe's, even without the dancing serve. He stopped looking for the ceiling and played the kind of control I had seen him use in Brooklyn. I was clearly outclassed, but fired up. I was ready for the tiebreaker, but Abe protested that he was bushed, even though I could see that he hadn't even broken a sweat. There is room for compassion and generosity in handball. We cleaned up and headed home.

I expected Abe to go on to big tournament successes, but he never did. Instead, he went off and got married to a lovely woman. I was happy for him. His wife was charming, attractive, and energetic. She was athletic, too. A good match, it seemed. Except that she was a devoted square dancer. I don't know whether Abe knew of this awful flaw before they married or whether, in the glow of new love, he thought it could all be worked out. It started innocently enough, but it was an insidious process. He protested at first that he had two left feet and couldn't possibly be a dancer.

"Oh," she crooned, "an athlete like you? Of course you can square-dance. Just give it a try."

She appealed to his vanity: He was so graceful. Any fine athlete would surely also be a fine dancer. His years of handball had prepared him for dancing. At first they danced on Wednesdays and Sundays and he played handball the other days. Soon they were planning special programs and needed another day or two for rehearsal. Then she bought him a red bandanna and he bought himself a corduroy shirt, and I knew it was all over. Not only did they dance, now they were instructors. Soon the nights were all consumed and Abe fell away from the path of righteousness. He set aside his gloves and cancelled his subscription to *Handball Magazine*.

In a few months, Abe will be back in Minneapolis, this time with his wife. They'll be attending a national square dance convention. They give master classes all over the country. They live in Florida now, where the dance season is longer. Abe wrote and invited me to their demonstration, but how can I attend? It chokes me up to think of what a champion he might have been. The dancing I want to see is on that wicked left-handed serve, not with a bandanna and a corduroy shirt.

Then again, maybe I'll go. I'll mention the new world-class handball courts that have recently been built on campus, and I'll mention the trouble I've been having with my back wall return. I'll ask for a few tips. I'll suggest that with all of his square dancing in recent years he should have great stamina and might be better than ever on the handball court. Now that he's been married for awhile, I'll bet his wife would be happy for him to go off on his own occasionally.

Meanwhile, I'm sticking with the Perfect Game. Right now, I'm the imperfect keeper of the family heritage. But I'm not giving up on Abe. I'll go to that demonstration and, if it's necessary, I may even dance a step or two. Don't worry about me, though. I've got two left feet.

# The Spirit Endureth

THIS IS FOLLY! I have no business in this locker room, dressing to play singles against Rick Hall. After a hard day's work filled with insoluble problems, I don't need further humiliation. Rick is almost twenty-five years younger than I am. A weight lifter, he's stronger than I ever was, and he's a better athlete as well. I've played a lot more handball and ought to be smarter, but what good is experience when you can no longer execute?

A year ago Rick was a newcomer, eager to learn the game. He'd played a little in the Marines but there hadn't been much competition and he switched to karate—brown belt. His service commitment completed, he came back to school. That's where I met him, in the locker room here at the University of Minnesota. He saw the gloves and decided to try handball again.

Of course I encouraged him—the handballer's code. I patiently brought him along, nurtured him, and applauded his efforts without lording it over him. You'd think he would be grateful.

The first month or two he flailed around the court, while, with uncanny accuracy, I hit the ball hither when he was yon, and so on. He didn't give me much of a game at first, but I didn't mind, knowing in my heart that I was bringing another young person into the handball fraternity.

That phase didn't last very long. He was soon putting hither and yon together while my pinpoint accuracy unaccountably started to fail. Rick was hitting everything too hard and didn't have much of a mixture of shots, but he got points on sheer exuberance and hustle, and the scores were getting closer.

Then the worst possible thing happened. Fred, another handballer, hurt his right shoulder. Rather than give up the game, Ferocious Fred started playing one-handed and the rest of us accommodated—the handball code again—by also playing him with the off hand. That was truly unfortunate. Not for Fred, but for me. Two months of concentrated practice with the left hand was all that young Rick needed to round him out into a fine player. He was getting left-handed kills and passing shots while I was getting bone bruises and shoulder aches. The activity with the left hand seems to have unlocked the previously dormant handball center in the right side of his brain. (There is scientific evidence for the existence of such a center in the right cerebral cortex, in the parietal region.) Rick began mixing up his shots instead of overpowering everything and he began to play smart. All my instruction began to take hold. That's when the tide turned for good and it began taking me longer and longer to get dressed to play when Rick was my opponent.

Here I am again in the locker room, not moving too swiftly. Of course, it does take me awhile to get ready. I have to bandage my right foot because of the osteomyelitis I had as a child. Doc Priest told me recently it's a miracle I'm walking on that leg, to say nothing of playing ball. Then I have to put on the elbow bandage and the pads. I've got some cartilage floating around the right elbow, probably from slamming into the wall one too many times. Since last year I've been wearing eyeglasses. (You can only go so far in this game by a sense of smell, especially with some of the partners I play with.)

I can't even beat Rick in the locker room. He gets there fifteen minutes after me and is soon prancing up and down like a heavyweight waiting for the bell, while I'm struggling to pull my high-topped sneaker over my bandaged foot. Then we've got to walk down that long corridor to the court. The kid dances on ahead, then comes back for me, doing jumping jacks the whole time. He's limbering while I'm lumbering. During warm-ups, I lob the ball to the front wall, groaning when I have to reach down to retrieve it, and Rick pounds the ball with both hands without letting it hit the floor.

Last week I thought he was going to tear up the court just because I was winning the first of three games. I dropped in a few good serves and a few right-hand kills—I'm not too bad from close up—and he started talking to himself, loudly and with indelicate language. Then he put a good serve to my right that I miraculously managed to retrieve and returned, right into the middle of his back, a pure accident. Then he put another serve in the same location, with the same result. Really, it was like he was hitting himself, not me hitting him. All I could manage on those serves was the angle he gave me, which by the operation of the laws of physics ended up in the curve of his back. On the next play, I reached back behind me for a tough shot and caught Rick in the eye, right through the protective eye guard I had insisted he wear. It was a freak accident but Rick went ballistic. He pulled off the eye guard, slammed it to the floor, and uttered some deeply felt expletives. I'm happy to say there was no injury; Rick cooled down eventually and we finished the game. He even put on the eye guard again, which has nothing to do with the fact that I won that game.

So here I am in the locker room again, getting ready to play Rick. For the life of me I can't see why he should get upset when I win a game. He ought to be pleased that an older person like me can still play well occasionally. I don't figure that it violates the laws of nature for me to win a couple of handball games, calling on my years of experience and savvy. There's more to this game than good legs and brawn. I may be older, but I'm not ready for the old folks' home. Now that I think about it, I can't wait for our next game. I'm not going to lie down and quit because he can run and dive and make a few good saves. Agility is part of the game, but there are also some tricks you don't learn off the back of a Wheaties box. Let him run and dive. I'll have him running himself silly. I'll have him running hither while I put the ball yon. I'll....

*"Rick. Hi. Yeah, I'll be ready in a minute. I've just got to finish bandaging my foot and then I've got to clean my eyeglasses and put on my elbow guards. Sure I'm ready to play. Eager to. Raring to go. C'mon and get your stuff on. I don't want to lose any court time waiting for you."*

# Winning Isn't Everything

SOMETIMES WEEKS GO BY during which I can't seem to put together a winning handball game. Recently I've been receiving ignominious treatment from both ends of the age spectrum. Joe Dodds is only twenty-three and Col. Fred Adelman may have served in the Boer War. Both have been whipping me soundly. This is very bad for my morale and my self-image. At times like this, when I can't seem to win a game, I sometimes think about playing Harvey again.

I first met Harvey at a mutual friend's house and discovered that we were both handball enthusiasts. It didn't take long before we were locked in locker-room conversation, ignoring the other guests, swapping stories about the great ones we had seen or heard about, demeaning our own prowess, trying to get a sense of how formidable an opponent the other would be. Harvey invited me to his club and within a week I was putting on my handball gear, wondering whether I had gotten in over my head with this tough New York street fighter who still had the jungle instincts.

While I bandaged my right foot, I casually mentioned that I'd had osteomyelitis as a child and had a great deal of pain in that foot. Harvey retorted that he had broken his ankle on the court less than a year ago; this would be the first real test of how well it had healed. Score for Harvey. His broken ankle trumped my much older injury, especially since his had been sustained during a game.

"How did it happen?" I asked, not really wanting to hear.

"I was still in New York," he said, "playing with a fellow who always beat me. I had never even come close before, but I had a premonition—a kind of tingle—and I knew that this time would be different.

I dominated from the moment I entered the court. It was a marvelous feeling. I was indomitable."

He paused and seemed far away, recalling that glorious encounter. I finally intruded on his reverie. "What about your leg? How did you break your leg?"

Harvey reluctantly came back to the present. "It was my father. Nothing I had ever done or accomplished was sufficient for him. In his eyes I was always short of the mark. I grew up with the sure knowledge that success would always elude me. And there, on the court, just as I was building up a commanding lead with my brilliant play, my father's image loomed before me and I knew that I had to lose. But I couldn't lose because I was playing so well. So I broke my ankle."

"Are you trying to tell me that it was because of your father that you broke your ankle during that game?"

"Exactly. He had been dead for years, but I felt his presence, and his judgment. I couldn't win, but neither could I lose. I resolved my dilemma by breaking my ankle."

"You mean you purposely broke your ankle?"

"No, of course not. I don't have that kind of courage. I did it subconsciously. I couldn't deny my father. Nor could I deny myself at that moment. My psychiatrist agrees with my analysis and thinks it quite clever."

I followed Harvey onto the court reluctantly, his story running through my mind. He insisted that he was ready to play and had resolved his physical and emotional problems. I tried to put him off. Perhaps his leg wasn't quite healed. Shouldn't he have another visit to the doctor? Harvey would hear none of it. He had assurances from his psychiatrist. And recently he had taken up transcendental meditation. He was ready. I asked him to let me know instantly if his father appeared during the game.

I had no notion of how to approach the contest. Should I try to beat him, and perhaps ravage his self-respect? Or should I let him win and chance his father's vengeful spirit? How well could he play? Perhaps the combination of mystic tingle, psychiatric care, and transcendental meditation would prove too much for me and I would have no choice in the end.

We began playing and it soon became evident that either Harvey was a much poorer player than I had expected, or this was an elaborate ruse. He stumbled around the court, hitting the ball only occasionally. He crashed into the walls going for simple shots and groaned loudly. He looked as though he might expire and I became alarmed.

"Are you all right? Look, why don't we just practice a little today and play another time, after you've gotten back into condition?"

"No, I'll play," Harvey uttered through clenched teeth. "If only this damned leg doesn't give out again."

He was no competition. I made point after point. His breathing became labored and his face florid. He emitted awful sounds of agony, but refused to quit. I decided to beat him as quickly as possible and take us both out of his misery. Perversely, just as I approached the last point he suddenly came alive and successfully volleyed a few shots—before sagging, near exhaustion.

"Enough, Harvey," I called out. "Let's quit so that we can play another time."

He was not ready to stop, and he had one last surprise for me.

"Let's… finish…. But… wait… one… minute. … I… have… I… have… to… call… on… my… inner… resources…"

Now what? He looked prayerfully upward and began some sort of incantation. After a few moments, he took a deep breath and signaled that he was ready. It worked. He dashed after my serve, smashed the ball back, went rushing to the wall for another return, and then—collapsed. The game ended and Harvey stumbled off the court. After a long shower, he could finally speak.

"You see," he said mournfully, "it's just as I told you. It's my father. He can't bear to see me succeed."

"Sure, Harvey, sure." I agreed eagerly, grateful that his color and breathing were returning to normal. "We'll play again. But maybe you should take it easy for awhile, build up gradually."

For the next few days I half expected to hear some dreadful news about Harvey, but he survived. A few weeks later I received a telephone call from a sophisticated sounding secretary.

"Mr. Siegel? I am Mr. H's personal secretary. He asked me to arrange an engagement at his club at your earliest convenience. When might you be available?"

"Oh," I responded heartily, "I am *terribly* sorry, but I am swamped with work this week, for the next several weeks, as a matter of fact. Perhaps later in the year…"

There were several follow-up calls, but I declined all further invitations. I like to win, but not that badly. There simply is no room for me on a court already crowded with Harvey, his father, his psychiatrist, and his guru. I'll take my chances with Joe Dodds and the Colonel.

Winning isn't everything.

# Handball Hype

*(Editorial Note: In the 1980s the American Handball Association, under the sponsorship of Robert Kendler, developed a new "family handball" to replace the punishingly hard, black ball that had been used for generations. The new ball was bright blue and had a soft outer surface that was designed to make the game inviting to a larger audience of potential players, including women.)*

THE BOB KENDLER FAMILY handball will help educate the public to the fact that handball is the Perfect Game for everyone, and not merely for an elite group of macho men with hands of steel. The new blue ball is gentle to the touch and much less likely to bruise delicate hands. It is bound to attract men and women of all ages to the game. Equally important, handball has finally broken with the same dull, drab, black ball that has so long dominated the sport. The introduction of this comely blue ball heralds the start of a revolution in color and fashion for handball.

For decades handball has attracted athletes because of the superb workout, the test of skill and endurance, the classic confrontation between brawn and brain. These are noble attributes, but there is a dimension to the game that has been shamefully ignored. To make the Perfect Game even more perfect, handball needs a change in attire, a dress code, a fashion statement.

Think back to the time when you first brought a loved one to watch a handball game. Recall how she had to slither past sweaty bodies in torn, grubby sweatshirts, shorts of every color except one that matched the shirt, nondescript socks, and tattered, discolored sneakers. Of perfume I need say nothing. Contrast this lamentable costume with the sartorial perfection of the tennis player, the simple tastefulness of a baseball uniform. When a baseball player smudges his uniform, he immediately rushes to the dugout for a new one. Football players continually pat each other on the rump to brush away dirt or grime. A basketball player would be booted off the court if he dribbled on his jersey. Why should less be expected of handball players?

The family blue ball is a bold start, but let us not stop there. Let us have handballs of yellow, chartreuse, purple, peppermint bonbon. And let us insist on uniforms that coordinate shoes, socks, shorts, shirts, and sweatbands. Indeed, let us go one layer deeper, for who can predict when a pair of shorts will split at the seam as a player flings himself around the court. Opponents should check with each other before a match to be assured that their outfits will not clash.

In the new era of handball, players should take a few minutes between games to freshen up and change uniform. A player who is winning might select a cheerful pastel. If he is playing badly, a more muted outfit might seem more fitting. Gloves should be changed not when they become wet, but when they lose their fresh, aristocratic look. The knee or ankle bandage should be considered part of the player's wardrobe, chosen to complement the socks and shoes. The possibilities for eyewear are terribly exciting. Given an attractive variety of colors and shapes, even the most reluctant player will find eye guards irresistible. Indeed, the prescription eyeglasses of the future may well be fashioned to mimic the new, chic handball eye guards. For the handball athlete, a high fashion gym bag would be the perfect gift, perhaps with his or her initials set neatly in needlepoint.

A dress and fashion code for handball will open all kinds of new opportunities for our champions. Our heroes will finally get the recognition they deserve and will be asked to endorse all kinds of products. Oh, you handball players, cast off your old, worn, tattered gym clothes. *Handball Magazine* will never again feature a drab, brown, crusty pair of gloves. The future is at hand, handballers. Do not drop the ball. Take advantage of the special introductory outfits that will be featured in subsequent issues of this magazine. Look for those outfits to be appealingly modeled by this year's pro tour when they arrive in your city. Clip out the order form, send us your vital statistics, and let us do the rest. Be sure to specify your hair and eye color and to describe your complexion. We will send you an individually styled uniform that will take your breath away. Be the first in your club to sport the new Handball Fashion Coordinates and make a contribution to your own lifestyle, as well as to the great game of handball.

# From the Pulpit

# Vayera
## (Genesis 22: 1–24)

THE PASSAGE WE READ today, often referred to as the Akedah, or the Binding, begins with the statement that God put Abraham to the test: God orders Abraham to offer his son Isaac in sacrifice—Isaac, who was to be the conduit through which the covenant would be realized, the culmination of Abraham's wanderings, and the hope of his old age. Abraham is told to bring Isaac to an altar somewhere in the obscure land of Moriah, there to be offered as a human sacrifice.

Abraham faithfully carries out God's instructions and brings Isaac to the edge of death, but at the last instant, Isaac is saved—by God, the Redeemer Who gives and sustains life. The covenant is affirmed and renewed. Speaking through an angel, God declares:

> By Myself I swear, because you have done this and have not withheld your son, your favorite one, I will bestow My blessing upon you and make your descendents as numerous as the stars of heaven and the sands on the seashore (Genesis, 22: 16-17).

In this passage there is an unmistakable causal link: God reaffirms the covenant because Abraham was faithful and obedient. Abraham is tested, he passes the test, and we Jews of later generations reap the rewards.

All of us who have at one time been teachers or students might recognize that there is something in this interpretation of the Akedah that doesn't ring true. In a test, there are two possible outcomes: pass or fail. As I read the *Parasha*, however, there was no possibility that Abraham could fail.

To illustrate my point, let us suppose that Abraham's love for his son had overwhelmed his obedience. Suppose that, when he heard God's command, Abraham had said:

No, I will not bring Isaac to the place You will show me. I will not cause the child to carry the means of his destruction on his own back. No, I will not bind the child and look into his terrified eyes. I will not draw the knife to slay my son. Dear God, I dare not acquiesce in this because if I do, not only Isaac, but I too will be destroyed, and who will be left to honor and magnify Your Name? I cannot perform this sacrifice because You are a God of mercy and justice, and I must strive to make Your ways my ways.

If Abraham had refused to carry out God's command, he still would have earned an A+ on the test. In their first encounter (Genesis12:2), God promised Abraham that He would make a great nation of his seed, and He did not have Ishmael in mind. God chose Abraham unconditionally for this historic role of nation-building. God was bound by His own covenant. If Abraham had refused to sacrifice Isaac, he still would have found favor in God's eyes, and God might then have said: "Because you have done this and have *withheld* your son, I will bestow My blessing on you and make your descendents as numerous as the stars of heaven and the sands of the seashore."

If Abraham understood that God did not truly require the sacrifice of Isaac, we may ask why he proceeded to carry out God's command. He did so not out of blind faith or mindless obedience. The test was not whether Abraham loved God more than Isaac. Such a test is unthinkable and impossible. If Abraham had to show his love for God by destroying his child, that very act of love would have been a repudiation of God.

I suggest that in refusing to deny God, Abraham was probing God's intent, testing the meaning of God's mercy and justice. When Abraham arose early that morning and put the kindling on Isaac's back, and when Isaac remained silent in the face of these ominous events, Isaac and Abraham pushed God to the limits of His resolve. How long could God suffer to see Abraham and Isaac suffer? In the end, God relented; it was God, not Abraham, who chose the ram in place of Isaac. God's compassion could not be restrained. In this test of loyalty, Abraham and Isaac prevailed, and surely God must have rejoiced.

In submitting to God, Abraham and Isaac deepened our understanding of God's will. We know that God would not—could not—accept Isaac in sacrifice and could not bear to see Abraham grieve. We learn that God would not allow the history of the Jewish people to falter. It is with this understanding of the Akedah that I approach these Days of Awe and beseech the God of Abraham and Isaac to teach us the ways of charity, mercy, compassion, and loving-kindness that were revealed during the binding. May it be so in this season and all the seasons of our lives.

Shabbat Shalom!

# Vayishlach
## (Genesis 32:4 – 36:43)

MY NAME IS YAAKOV, and I have a limp, and I almost didn't make it this morning. I was up half the night wrestling, not with an angel, but with Jacob—or rather, with the story of Jacob. Today's *Parasha* deals with momentous events in the life of Jacob, and it left me puzzling about Jacob's names. In one of the most dramatic episodes in the Torah, Jacob, after pleading with God for his own safety and for the safety of his family, wrestles through the night with a mysterious stranger. Some commentators suggest the stranger is Esau's evil angel; others, more to my liking, see the stranger as God's messenger; still others consider the angel to be Jacob's own destructive impulses that he needs finally to bring under control. The struggle occurs when Jacob has separated himself from his wives and children. He never sees the face of his adversary and never learns his name. He is alone and surrounded by darkness. There is no one to cheer him on, no one to call out, "Go, Jake. You can do it!" This is a personal, not a public struggle.

We learn that Jacob wins the match, though only after suffering a wound to his thigh, and that as daylight approaches, he coerces a blessing from the angel, who says: "You shall no longer be Jacob, but Israel, for you have striven with beings divine and human, and have prevailed."

Jacob is now *Israel*—the name has resonated through the ages and we, the descendents of Jacob, have appropriated it for our own. A little later, after Jacob has met and reconciled with his brother Esau, God appears to Jacob, blesses him, and certifies the change in name.

God says (35:10): "You whose name is Jacob, you shall be called Jacob no more, but Israel shall be your name."

The angel is not only God's messenger, he is also in charge of naming rights. After losing the battle to Jacob, the angel draws up a name-change contract, gets it notarized and signed by God. Jacob is no longer to be known as a deceiver, haunted by events in his past. Our hero, our namesake, has passed on to a new stage in his life and has been granted a new name in recognition of the achievement.

But there is a problem: Just a few verses later (35:14) we read that "Jacob set up a pillar at the site where God had spoken to him…" Whoops! What happened to Israel? God has just said, "You shall no longer be Jacob," but in the text, it is Jacob who sets up the pillar, not Israel. Could the Torah, like me, be having trouble remembering names after a only few thousand years?

That's my puzzle. Why would the Torah record that God changed Jacob's name, and then revert almost immediately to his original name? There are other name changes in the Torah, but once applied, they stick. When Avram becomes Abraham, that's his name from then on. The same is true of Sarai, once she becomes Sarah. The new names reflect their changed situation, and there is no possibility that they will go back to their old status and their old names.

Names are powerful. Jacob's wrestling partner will not reveal his name; nor will God, not even to Abraham or Moses. In the mystic tradition, the Baal Shem Tov was called the Master of the Good Name and he used God's mysterious names to heal and bring peace to others. Shakespeare could write, "What's in a name? That which we call a rose by any other name would smell as sweet," but those lines are spoken by a young, love-struck, and naïve child whose life will end tragically. In the Torah names of places and names of people are rich with meaning and implication.

That brings me back to my puzzle: Why does the Torah refer to Jacob by his old name even after God has anointed him "Israel"? For that matter, why do we call on Jacob and not Israel when we pray the *Amidah* (the central prayer of the Jewish liturgy)? And, more important, why did my mother confuse everybody by naming me "Gerald" with a G and "Jerry" with a J? But that's a matter for another sermon.

Is there a pattern? Is Jacob always doing something noble when he is called Israel, but less honorable when he is Jacob? I don't find that, but I do think that the Torah intends to teach us something by the way that Jacob's names vary. I think the lesson may be that even after "prevailing over beings divine and human," the real struggle isn't over for Jacob. His redemption and transformation are not complete.

We see a progression in Jacob in just the way he accumulates blessings. At first, he captures his father's blessing by deceit, by pretending to be Esau. In today's *Parasha*, he receives a blessing by physical coercion, by refusing to free the angel as daybreak approaches. But later in the *Parasha*, when God confirms his new name as Israel, God's blessing is offered spontaneously, without Jacob asking or struggling. At that point, he has earned it.

I think the Torah wants us to understand that even after receiving God's blessing, Jacob has work to do—to become a more honest, understanding person, to learn to deal evenly and fairly with his children, and to have the sobering experience of great sadness and loss. Jacob, after all, is human, and the job of becoming Israel, of prevailing over his own failings and worst impulses, is not accomplished in one night's heroic struggle. Our sages knew that the battle with the *yetzer harah*, the evil inclination, is the work of a lifetime.

In these respects, Jacob is not so different from us, as we attempt to grow in maturity and wisdom and to deal with our personal imperfections. During the High Holy Days we recall and express our regrets for the sins we have accumulated over the past year, and we vow to do better. Yom Kippur is not a once in a lifetime event. It comes around every year because, despite our hopes and best intentions, we fall short and we sin again. Yom Kippur is the gift that keeps on giving because it acknowledges our human fallibilities and also our capacity for improvement.

In Genesis 49, Jacob blesses his sons in the most extraordinary way, reciting their sins as well as their virtues, and prophesying their futures. The Torah tells us that when Jacob finished his instructions to his sons, he was gathered to his people, to join Abraham, Sarah, Isaac, Rebecca, and Leah in the cave of Machpelah. Even then, the circle of his life is touched by sadness because Rachel, most beloved of all, was buried elsewhere and was not there to greet him.

Joseph and his brothers buried Jacob, not Israel, in the cave of Machpelah, because Israel still has work to do, work that we sometimes refer to as "tikkun olam." The Torah points to what is required. Jacob is named *Israel* just as he is finally about to confront his past and make peace with Esau, the brother he wronged twenty years earlier. In the Amidah prayer, perhaps we invoke Jacob's name because he was all too human and we hope that if God could look past his frailties, we too will be forgiven and blessed. In the Shema, however, we say "Shema Yisrael…" because it is Israel who must hear and understand. We have inherited Jacob's struggle. We, like Jacob, will truly become Israel when we grasp a brother's heel to lift him up, not to hold him back, when we set aside our differences and learn to live with one another in peace, when we make the Torah a living force in our lives as we go about the unfinished business of tikkun olam.

And then, you angels, if you think Jacob could wrestle, watch what we can do!

Shabbat Shalom!

# Beha'alotecha
## (Numbers 8:1–12:16)

SIXTY-ONE YEARS AGO on this date in the Jewish calendar, I celebrated my Bar Mitzvah, in Brooklyn, New York, and the *Parasha* that Shabbat was Beha'alotecha. As was the practice in those days, I didn't read Torah, only the Haftarah. I gave a speech in Yiddish that I had memorized and didn't understand, and afterwards I was showered with little packets of raisins and nuts, thrown down by the women from the balcony above.

After the services we had an open house in our small apartment, and neighbors and relatives gathered to congratulate me and to feast on the corned beef, pastrami, and salami supplied by our friend Abie Lederman, who was in the delicatessen business and could get it wholesale. During the festivities we ran out of bread. My mother gave me a dollar and sent me to Kessler's bakery on the corner of Seventy-seventh Street and Eighteenth Avenue. I'd scarcely reached the front stoop when I was stopped by Tante Rifka, my aunt from the Bronx. We didn't see Tante Rifka often, but when she visited she invariably criticized her sister Annie, my grandmother, for raising children and grandchildren with so little commitment to Jewish observance. She was my religious and cranky aunt.

There she was at my Bar Mitzvah, standing on the stoop, not quite five feet tall but nonetheless a giant, barring my way as I set out for the bakery clutching the dollar my mother had given me. Tante Rifka saw the money in my hand and was horrified.

"What are you doing?' she said.

"Mom sent me to the bakery."

"On the Shabbos of your Bar Mitzvah. *Vos far a Yid bist du?* What kind of a Jew are you? You can't do that. Give me that money!"

Before I could answer, she snatched the dollar from my hand and disappeared. Not long afterward she was back, carrying a package. She had gone to the store herself and bought the bread. It wasn't until years later that I realized what an extraordinary sacrifice this deeply religious, and very cranky, woman had made on my behalf, violating the Sabbath so that I would not.

Extraordinary (and cranky) men and women like my Tante Rifka are part of our heritage, as we learn from today's *Parasha*. Just a short time after experiencing the plagues, escaping from slavery, witnessing the wonders at the Red Sea and at Mt. Sinai—with all that still fresh in memory—our ancestors began complaining about the desert cuisine. They forgot about their suffering in Egypt. They wanted corned beef sandwiches, with a pickle on the side. They accosted Moses bitterly: "If only we had meat to eat!…our gullets are shriveled. There is nothing at all! Nothing but this manna to look to!"

Moses couldn't call on Abie Lederman to satisfy the craving of these ungrateful people. Instead, he did what any good Jew does in an impossible situation—he also complained, bitterly and directly to God. The conversation is recorded in the Torah:

Where am I to get meat to give all this people, when they whine before me and say, "Give us meat to eat!".… If You would deal thus with me, kill me rather, I beg You, and let me see no more of my wretchedness (Numbers, 11:13-15).

"Kill me!" These are strong words. This is championship level *kvetching* (complaining), but it works. God tells Moses He will personally do the catering. The Israelites will have so much meat they will choke on it until it comes out of their nostrils. And God also proposes a committee of seventy elders to help Moses as his management team.

We modern Jews know that Moses should be worrying about the committee meetings but instead he is still obsessing about the meat. Where are You going to get enough meat, he says, to satisfy six hundred thousand men (he only mentions the men; remember, the women were in the balcony). Imagine! Moses questions God's power to create a small-type miracle—the sort the synagogue kitchen staff do week after week.

The God we encounter in Numbers is quixotic and unpredictable; sometimes angry, even enraged, ready to turn away from the people He has chosen. At other times, He is gracious and forgiving. In this instance, God forgives Moses. Later, however, when Moses disobeys God and brings water from a rock by striking rather than speaking to it, God is unforgiving and He forbids Moses from entering the Promised Land.

Throughout our long history we have been a stiff-necked people, argumentative, rebellious, kvetching, quarreling with our leaders and among ourselves, even to this day. We complain, but we remain; we kvetch, but we also stretch. Perhaps there is something redeeming even in our complaining,

Jacob vanquished the angel and became Israel, but his tribulations didn't end there. He limped along for the rest of his life, dealing with disappointments, never quite satisfied, nursing deep resentments, even when he was finally reunited with his beloved son Joseph. "My days have been short and bitter," he tells Pharaoh. We empathize with Jacob because, like us, he did not accomplish all he wished to, because he understood that God is a demanding and difficult partner, and because he knew that Israel's role in history would be challenging and often painful.

The Israelites that Moses led out of Egypt criticized him, questioned God, and complained for the forty years they wandered in the desert, and yet out of this rabble, there emerged a great nation. They couldn't find a short cut across the Sinai, but they developed an unprecedented moral compass, a yearning to study and learn, and a reverence for justice. They left us an inheritance—a compulsion to heal the world, which is both a blessing and a burden. "Tikkun olam" is a communal kvetch—an open admission that as Jews we are not satisfied with the world as we find it and are obligated to do something about it.

In the Torah and the commentaries, our own sacred books, our flaws are on display for all to see, and from time to time Moses and even God despairs of us. But we are also fated to become a holy nation and a light unto the world. In the very first lines of today's Torah portion, Moses and Aaron are given detailed instructions on crafting the menorah, the universal symbol of the Jewish people. I wondered why God should be so concerned with interior decorating— with how the menorah is fashioned, and just where it is placed. I think the message in these elaborate instructions is that God has chosen and placed us among the nations so that His presence will shine through us. But we are not passive receptacles that simply reflect the light. Through our heritage of Torah we are taught that the way to tikkun olam is through deeds of justice, compassion, and loving-kindness. That is how the light is disseminated. And if along the way we indulge in a little complaining, become a little argumentative, that wouldn't be entirely unexpected. As Moses, Jacob, the Prophets and, yes, my Tante Rifka have shown, kvetching is part of our heritage too.

Shabbat Shalom!

# Shlach L'cha
## (Numbers 13:1–15:41)

THE TORAH PORTION WE READ today ranges over a number of topics, including the practice of "taking challah." In Temple days, when bread was baked, the first loaf would be dedicated to God and given to the priest. Not long ago I received a call from a non-Jewish friend in Santa Fe. He had bought a box of Manischewitz matzos and noticed an inscription on the box that said, "Challah is taken." He wanted to know who had taken it and what challah had to do with matzos. After the destruction of the Temple, the Rabbis decreed that as a symbol of this ancient practice, a piece of the dough should be thrown into the oven before the first loaf is baked. Kosher bakers continue this practice.

Of course, the story of the twelve spies is the most compelling part of today's *Parasha*. Like so much of Torah, what seems at first to be a simple case of good and evil, sin and punishment, turns out to raise many complex problems. For me, the questions that finally emerged dealt not with the spies, but with my own relationship to God.

As *Parasha* Shlach L'Cha begins, the Israelites have been traveling in the desert for two years since the exodus from Egypt. Conditions have been harsh. I imagine days that were often unbearably hot and evenings that brought bone-chilling cold. The Israelites travel on foot. There have been shortages of water. The menu has not been to their liking. They no longer remember their suffering in Egypt and how they cried to God to take them out of bondage. Now they think of Egypt with fondness and express the wish to return. On several occasions God has been so provoked that He is ready to destroy these ungrateful people and create a whole new nation, but each time Moses appeals to God's compassion and mercy, and the people are spared.

At the moment this *Parasha* opens, however, things are looking up. After a stunning military victory at Arad, the Israelites are poised to invade Canaan. God is their constant companion; the Holy Ark is in their midst; there is every indication they will be blessed with victory and their long journey out of slavery will finally be ended. However, as is so often the story of our ancestors, triumph and celebration are replaced by disruption and tragedy.

Before attacking the Canaanites, Moses selects twelve men to scout out the land. He wisely selects one man from each tribe so there will be no whispers that he had favorites. The men he selects are chieftains—men of authority. Their names are recorded for all eternity in the Torah. They are not merely spies, they are God's emissaries. They are given the privilege of being the first of this community of former slaves to set foot on the holy ground that will be Israel's future.

The spies return after forty days and hold up a lush branch of grapes to show that the land is rich with produce, as God had promised. But then ten of the spies dash the people's spirits by announcing that the land is unconquerable. It is too heavily fortified. The residents are giants. It is hopeless. Caleb and Joshua disagree, but they are ignored. The Israelites once again fall into despair. They rail against Moses and Aaron, and clamor to return to Egypt.

God is incensed with the Israelites and their lack of faith. He decrees that this generation will not set foot in the Promised Land. They will wander in the desert for forty years with the bitter knowledge that they had been on the very threshold of deliverance. The punishment for the ten spies is even more harsh. They are all killed immediately and their names are now associated with treachery rather than honor.

That's the outline of the story: joy and anticipation give way to suffering and tragedy. For the next thirty-eight years, the Torah becomes silent. It is not until our people are finally ready once again to enter the land that the story picks up. Whatever pain or suffering or redemption occurred in those intervening years is not recorded.

# SHLACH L'CHA

Most of the commentaries I have read on this *Parasha* speculate on what it was about the behavior of the spies that warranted such extreme punishment. We take it as given that God metes out punishment that is proportionate to the crime. The spies must have been truly evil to deserve such a fate. We come to this conclusion because we cannot imagine that God does not act fairly and justly.

In our *Parasha* the spies are judged and sentenced, but something is missing. The Torah doesn't include testimony for the defense. We don't know whether they offered excuses for their behavior. We don't know why they responded as they did to what they saw. We don't know whether they repented or pleaded for mercy. For a moment, let's go beyond the text and imagine the arguments a defense lawyer might have presented out there in the desert to save his ten defendants.

The lawyer might have opened by recalling that the defendants hadn't requested this mission. They were recruited to it. Furthermore, these were men of good character. Moses himself is their character witness. They were selected because they could be trusted and were men of honor. They were leaders. Furthermore, they must have resisted the temptations of the golden calf. Otherwise, they would have perished with those who participated in that sin. So, they were not devious or dishonest men at the outset.

The spies scouted different parts of the land. Ten came back with the same dismal report. To indict all ten suggests that they were in some sort of conspiracy; that they were guilty of collusion. But there is no hint in our *Parasha* that they jointly fabricated a story that would strike fear in the hearts of the others. Next week, when we hear the case of Korah, we will learn of a rebellion against the leadership of Moses and Aaron that was clearly a grab for power. But no such motive for the spies appears in this week's text.

Instead of attributing evil impulses to these men, let me suggest that the spies were flawed individuals, but not traitors. Let me suggest that they truly reported what they thought they saw. Their judgment was clouded. They were frightened, perhaps even cowardly, but these are emotions, not sins and not crimes. To them, the inhabitants seemed enormous, and the land unconquerable. They ignored the miracles God had already made for them in bringing them out of Egypt and they failed to take God's overwhelming power into account as they assayed their chances of success, but they weren't sent out to describe God's power; that was not their job. If the agenda was to come back with a favorable report, and only a favorable report, there was no reason to send them out in the first place.

Their words had a devastating effect on the others, but should the spies be blamed for the weakness of the people? The Israelites were constantly complaining and threatening to return to Egypt. They made Moses' life a misery and drove God to distraction. The Israelites could have taken their cues from Joshua and Caleb. They could have remembered all the miracles that had been done on their behalf. Why punish the messengers for defects in the people who received the message?

And finally, if I was their defense attorney, I would plead that these ten spies be spared the death sentence. Look at what punishment they've already received. Their names will always be associated with God's anger. Let them live out their lives and die in the desert with the others.

God and I have a difference of opinion here, and it is this difference that brought me to think about my relationship to God. Do we dare question God's justice? I think we wouldn't be Jews if we did not. Jacob struggled with God and became Israel. And we, the children of Israel, also struggle with God. We struggle when we try to understand the true nature of the spies' sin; we struggle with God when we grieve over the fate of Aaron's sons; when we ponder why He afflicted Job; when we contemplate the mystery of why bad things happen to good people, in Rabbi Kushner's words; or when we wonder how God could speak out of a burning bush, and yet remain silent during the flames of the Holocaust.

It is part of our tradition to question and to challenge God. When God was ready to destroy all Israel in his anger over the spies, Moses repeated God's own words, reminding God that He is "… slow to anger and abounding in kindness; forgiving iniquity and transgression." When God proposed to destroy Sodom and Gomorrah, Abraham challenged Him. We hold God to a high standard. We apprehend God in His own image, the image that is found in the Torah. God is just, generous, gracious, forgiving, merciful; God delights in our *tshuvah*, in our repentance. This is the God that I find in the Torah, and God, like us, is bound by His Torah.

I have a book at home that was sent to me by a former student who wanted to share the good news of her own religious conversion to messianic Christianity. The purpose of the book is to convince Jews that our religion has been supplanted by Christianity. As an example of how Judaism is flawed, the author cites the Talmudic story in which several rabbis have a dispute over a religious ruling—about whether a certain oven is kosher. Rabbi Eliezer calls on God to arbitrate the dispute but Rabbi Joshua responds that the dispute is "not in heaven." It is for us here, on earth, to bring the Torah into our own lives. The Talmud goes on to say that God, who witnessed this encounter, laughed and said, "My children have bested me." To the student who sent me the book, this story shows that Judaism is a failed religion, first because the rabbi dared to challenge God; and second because we imagine that God would take delight in such questioning. And yet it is precisely because of episodes like this that Judaism should be cherished, as a religion of the mind as well as the heart.

There are some who would react with consternation to my defense of the spies. They might say, "God's judgment is recorded in the Torah; no more need be considered. God's ways are not for us to question." But I don't believe that is what our tradition teaches. When I question God, I confront myself, I spy on myself, and my own deepest values, values that are brought to light in the Torah itself. I believe that makes me a better and more understanding Jew, and perhaps that's what God intended all along.

Shabbat Shalom!

# Shlach L'cha
## (Numbers 13:1–15:41)

TODAY'S *PARASHA* AND HAFTARAH are full of stories about spies: good spies and bad spies. Spies who see a land ripe for the taking and spies who see only defeat and destruction. Spies who find favor in God's eyes and spies who are doomed. Spies who cause decades of hardship and spies who lead the way finally to the Promised Land.

As a child, I grew up surrounded by spies. From the second floor in our Brooklyn apartment on Seventy-seventh Street, Mrs. Tannenbaum spied on me as I played street games with the other kids on the block; and when she was otherwise occupied, it was Mrs. Reiff on the first floor, or Mrs. Namowitz or Mrs. Fierberg from across the street. Any infraction was immediately reported to my mother, the disciplinarian in my family. Our Brooklyn neighborhood was like a small village, and any mischief—or thought of mischief—was broadcast far and wide, eventually ending in my mother's ears and a different part of my anatomy.

My grandmother Annie was also a spy, but a benevolent one who saved my hide on more than one occasion. If, by an act of God, and surely no fault of mine, I tore my trousers trying to reach second base in a punchball game, Grandma Annie would come to my rescue. And when my mother's punishment for some infraction became too enthusiastic, my grandmother would intervene. I suspect that most of us in this sanctuary are here because of the courage and tenacity of spies—parents or grandparents who left their homes in far-off lands to spy out America, the *Goldene Medina*, the golden land. They didn't speak English. They settled in neighborhoods that bore no resemblance to the *shtetls* or cities they had left behind, except perhaps for the familiar taste of poverty.

That generation who first set foot on Ellis Island could easily have concluded that America was unconquerable, that they were like grasshoppers, assaulted by a babble of languages and dialects they couldn't understand, surrounded by giants on teeming streets that were saturated with toil and sweat. They could have reached the same conclusion as the ten spies in today's *Parasha*. But our grandparents and great-grandparents were like Caleb and Joshua. Despite the hardships, they saw the opportunities in this new land even though they were squeezed together in overcrowded tenements, working long hours at low-paying jobs, often in unsafe conditions. They were determined to survive for their children and grandchildren.

They told jokes and wrote songs about their troubles— *"Es iz tsu mir gekumen a kuzine; sheyn vi gold iz zi geveyn, di grine….."* A beautiful, happy, spirited cousin came to America with glowing cheeks and feet that wished only to dance, until, alas, she was forced to work in a millinery shop. It's a funny, lively song that is sung with gusto, and the cheerful melody belies the sad message in the words. In the end this *grine kuzine* summarizes her feelings about her new home: *"Az brenen zol Kolumbes's medine!!!"* May a fire consume this land of Columbus. They sang this song at weddings and gatherings, making fun of their suffering, and at the same time they encouraged their relatives to come—come to America.

Our Biblical ancestors, about whom we read in today's *Parasha*, were slaves who knew little about freedom. It is easy to disparage them. In the Book of Numbers, they repeatedly disappoint God and Moses: they worship a golden idol right after experiencing the revelation at Sinai; they question Moses' leadership; they complain about the cuisine—the manna is too bland, too spicy, too salty, too greasy, not like the gourmet food they had in Egypt—they lose heart just as they are poised to enter Canaan. Time after time Moses has to plead with God not to destroy this stiff-necked people.

Despite their flaws, which are well documented in the Torah, these are the same Israelites who built the Tabernacle, giving generously of their own possessions and talents. In today's *Parasha*, they hear from God that they will never reach the Holy Land. Nonetheless, for another thirty-eight years they follow Moses and support him in fierce battles against enemies. They learn about festivals and holidays that they will not celebrate in the Land; about *kashrut, tzedakah,* and *Shabbat*. They learn of their obligations to each other and to strangers. And they teach their children about the degradations of slavery, and prepare them for a life of holiness. God's promise will be fulfilled in a place they will never reach, but still they persevere. Like our grandparents, they toil for the next generation.

We know a great deal about the twelve spies that Moses chose. God's anger consumes the ten who give an evil report, but they are brought back to life year after year as their names are read out in sacred congregations all over the world. This is their greatest punishment. All of us can hope our names will be remembered for a blessing. Not so for these ten. And yet, despite their awful fate, they can claim a certain victory. The irony in Shlach L'cha is that the disgraced spies were allowed to enter the land, to see how fertile and abundant it was, to taste its fruit, while Moses, Aaron, and Miriam died on the other side of the Jordan.

Perhaps we are to learn from this that our ways of measuring success and reward are too narrow. Moses does not enter the Promised Land, but if he had, that would be an individual reward, a personal achievement. Perhaps the Torah is teaching us that a more important accomplishment is to make it possible for others to succeed. The measure of Moses' greatness is that he brought the Israelites to a place physically, emotionally, and spiritually where they were finally ready to go on without him.

Like Moses, we all embark on journeys that we are not destined to complete. But that does not mean that we shouldn't have set forth, or that we have failed. In Pirke Avot (the Sayings of the Fathers) we learn from Rabbi Tarfon that "the day is short and the work is great," and that although we are not obligated to complete the work, we are also not free to desist from it. The work, I think, is tikkun olam. But there is more. We are not only obligated to do our own work of tikkun olam, we need also to prepare those who follow us to continue the work. We do that by the example of our deeds and by showing the next generation that there are great rewards for study and contemplation of Torah. Moses was followed by Joshua. That was no accident. He brought Joshua into the circle of his counsel and God's embrace. I was a university teacher for forty years and had great pleasure and pride in seeing my students set out on successful careers of their own. That is true of all teachers, and Moses was our greatest teacher. Of course the work doesn't end with us. If we have done well, we will have encouraged those who follow us to set out on their own journey of making the world a better place.

It's good to end on that hopeful note, but I also want to add a note of caution as we set off on our various journeys. Let's not forget that back in Brooklyn, Mrs. Tannenbaum, Mrs. Reiff, Mrs. Namowitz, and Mrs. Fierberg will be leaning out of their first- and second-story windows, observing, looking, ready to report any straying from the right path. I hope Grandma Annie will be there to rescue us.

Shabbat Shalom!

# Korah
## (Numbers 16:1-18:32)

THESE ARE HARD TIMES for our Israelite ancestors. Just last week in Shlach L'cha, they were poised to enter the Promised Land and do battle with the Canaanites, with Moses in the lead, the Ark in place, and God in their midst. Victory was in their grasp. But it all fell apart when ten of the spies came back with a terrifying report about the inhabitants of the land. The people lost their nerve and lashed out at Moses. Then, impetuously, some decided to invade Canaan after all, but without God's blessing, and they were slaughtered by the enemy.

The Book of Numbers that we have been studying is an instruction manual on how to annoy God. Time and again Moses has to plead with God not to wipe out the whole ungrateful mob and start with a new nation. Now God is really furious. He commands the Israelites to turn away from the Land that holds Jewish destiny, and to head into the desert on a pilgrimage that leads only to the grave: "Your children shall be wanderers in the wilderness forty years .... until your carcasses are consumed in the wilderness (Numbers, 14:32-33)." That is tough love!

We all know that we are going to die. But we are fortunate, I think, in not knowing how and when. And so we make plans for the future as though there will be a future. *Im yirtseh Hashem*—God willing, we say, we will be at a certain place at a certain time. Of course we will be at the Bar Mitzvah or the wedding or the nursery school graduation ceremony—we wouldn't miss it. We set dates, make appointments, knowing in the back of our minds that nothing is truly certain. *Der mentsh trakht, un got lakht* (We plan and God laughs)!

Our ancestors do not have the comfort of that uncertainty after God orders them back into the desert. They can't contemplate what they will have for dinner when they finally arrive in the Land of Milk and Honey. They know that they will never set foot in the Promised Land. Instead, they will live out their lives as vagabonds in the unforgiving desert. Can you imagine what that must have felt like? Would you build a house knowing it will collapse before you put a mezuzah on the doorpost, or enter a contest when the winner has already been chosen, or rent a tuxedo and get all dressed up for the prom knowing your date will leave with somebody else—wearing the corsage you bought for her? Why bother? We are called a stiff-necked people. Well, of course we are. It's in our blood. Those ancient Israelites had to be stubborn to continue on when they already knew how unhappily their journey was going to end.

Against this background, two groups rise up to challenge Aaron and Moses in today's Torah portion. Korah leads the charge. He is a cousin to Moses, Aaron, and Miriam. The prophet Samuel is a descendent, and Korah's children will go on to write many of the Psalms. He already has the high honor of serving as one of the carriers of the Ark. Despite his status and privileges, Korah wants more: he wants the priesthood. The second challenge comes from Dathan and Abiram. They want to displace Moses and become the leaders of the people. They are so cynical in their lust for power that they describe Egypt, where they endured terrible hardships, as a land of "milk and honey."

Moses is caught in a power struggle, with Korah emerging as the leader of the rebellion. Korah frames his arguments in lofty terms: You are all holy, he tells the people, stroking their vanity. Moses and Aaron are no better than you. Why should you accept their leadership when here I am, ready to be your servant? The Israelites have just learned they are destined to perish in the desert. They are distraught and unsettled, and Korah exploits their vulnerability.

Moses announces that God will settle the dispute. He tells Korah and his followers to lay incense on their fire pans and bring them in front of the holy Tabernacle. If this was playing at a Second Avenue Yiddish theater in New York, someone in the audience would yell out, "Don't do it, Korah. This is a trap! You are not an anointed priest, and God has forbidden anyone except the priests to make such offerings. Remember Aaron's sons who were incinerated for bringing 'false fire.'" But this is not Second Avenue, and Korah's ambition blinds him to danger. He has set his heart on the priesthood and nothing else matters. It is as though he thinks he is untouchable, even by God.

We all know people like this. John Edwards, a popular presidential contender, destroyed his marriage, his career, and almost went to jail. Bernie Madoff, one of our own, forfeited his future, damaged his family, and drove his son to suicide. Richard Nixon, Bill Clinton, Lyndon Johnson, all brilliant in their own way, tarnished their reputations and their legacies. We read of them in the Torah, too. The Torah is a casebook, a diagnostic manual, of human emotions, yearnings and passions.

The outcome of the contest is swift and terrible. God disposes of Korah, Dathan, Abiram and all who had joined them, in dramatic fashion—incinerated or swallowed alive by the earth. Tradition has it that their cries can still be heard from deep in the ground. Who needs Harry Potter? It's all here, in the Torah. The Israelites continue to grumble against Moses and Aaron, even after seeing this awesome destruction, and again God is ready to annihilate them all. Only fast action by Aaron saves them.

Our *Parasha* reads like a cautionary tale about how undeserving our ancestors were, how readily they were persuaded by the likes of Korah to rebel against Moses and God. Throughout the book of Numbers they are described as mutinous, unworthy of being God's chosen people. I think that judgment is too harsh.

In Egypt, generation after generation cried out to God, but there was no answer. Suddenly, Moses and Aaron appear out of nowhere and claim that they have been appointed by God to lead the Jews to freedom. As dreadful as their lives were under Pharaoh, they had learned to adapt and survive, and even keep a semblance of their Jewish identity. Now they are asked to give up known terrors for the unknown, and to follow a man who was living in Pharaoh's palace while they toiled in Egypt. This stranger shows up with God's private telephone number and Twitter address and tells the Israelites to fall in line. They didn't choose Moses and Aaron to be their leaders. They didn't elect them to office. It took hope, courage, and faith to sign on with these new leaders.

There were reasons for the people's grumblings in the desert. Even after they left Egypt, they weren't really free. They weren't slaves, but they were bound by strict rules that regulated their lives: Do not violate the Sabbath at pain of death. March when you are told to march, and rest when you are told to rest. Eat these foods, but not these others. Have absolute obedience to Moses and do not challenge his authority. Some of the rules promote justice, charity, and a civil society. Others are arbitrary and must be followed without questioning. And all of the rules were imposed rather than coming from the people. This is what was required of that generation of Jews.

Our ancestors can be faulted for their many lapses, but also admired for their endurance and stubborn instinct for survival. They continued to go forward even when they learned they would never reach their destination. They could have turned back, as they so often threatened. But despite their complaints they endured the hardships of the desert, did battle with the enemy, marched when they were told to march, and rested when they were told to rest.

Furthermore, during those years of wandering, they developed the characteristic that uniquely defines us to this day. They learned codes of behavior that would become the basis for all civil societies and they passed that passion for learning on to their children. This is a gift bequeathed to us by those ancient, stiff-necked Israelites.

On this Shabbat, we have studied the Torah of our ancestors' lives. With reverence, we pass the Torah from one generation to the next. The Torah is the beginning of wisdom, rich with potential for new understandings as we get more deeply into it. The written words of the Torah are the beginning of a conversation, not its conclusion. In our striving for a life of service and meaning, our Torah is the question, not the answer. That is why we also study the teachings of the rabbis—Talmud and Midrash—and why we are still studying, creating new Midrash, discovering new meanings. The questions raised in the Torah are eternal, and our answers only serve us for the moment, until our understandings deepen, and the questions deepen as well.

On this Shabbat we have experienced a remarkable time warp. It happens every Shabbat. We have been back in the desert with those ancient Israelites, and experienced that same Torah that Moses taught to our ancestors. May it always be so.

Shabbat Shalom!

# Balak
(Numbers 22:2—25:9)

AT FIRST READING, it may be difficult to keep track of the characters in today's *Parasha*. The action begins when Balak, king of the Moabites, becomes alarmed by the successes of the Israelites, and determines to find a way to defeat them. The weapon he chooses is Balaam, a prophet who presumably has the power to inflict curses on a people. Though the *Parasha* is called Balak, in ancient times it was probably known as "The Book of Balaam." Surely Balaam gets most of the good lines, and the *Parasha* pivots around his deeds, words, intentions, and motivations.

And what a complex character he is, a man of many contradictions: he is a pagan, and yet he speaks of *the Lord My God*, recognizing the God of Israel as his God, too. He is not Jewish, and yet God converses with him. He is a "seer" who supposedly can foretell the future, but can't see as well as his donkey. He sets out to curse God's chosen people. Instead, he blesses Israel in beautiful, poetic language—*How goodly are your tents, O Jacob, your dwellings, O Israel.*

The Torah, ordinarily a most serious document, sometimes surprises with its puns and wordplay, but the story of Balaam and his donkey is something rare, like a dour, humorless uncle suddenly telling an off-color joke. It's not clear whether the story should be read as Biblical entertainment—like the comic relief in Shakespeare's tragedies—or whether it contains a deeper message. Here is this famous prophet who, according to Balak, has the ability to change the course of history just by the words he utters; and yet, after he has repeatedly abused his faithful donkey, the animal loses patience and scolds him for being so blind. In fact, the donkey saves Balaam's life from a sword-wielding angel who was blocking his path and was ready to kill him.

Balaam doesn't express the slightest surprise that a dumb animal has suddenly started speaking. Instead, he and the donkey have a heated conversation about world affairs, and what to do when an angel is blocking the road. And the dignitaries traveling with Balaam express no surprise either. This, of course, is no ordinary animal. The only other animal to speak in the Bible is the snake that lured Eve into tasting that wonderful Honeycrisp apple in the Garden. Midrash explains that God created this donkey—or the donkey's mouth—on the eve of the first Shabbat of Creation and kept the miracle of its speaking in storage until this precise moment. The reason: because once Creation was completed, God didn't intend His miracles to violate the laws of nature, the very laws He put in place.

As the story unfolds, decisions are taken, and then reversed, and then reversed again. God tells Balaam not to go a'cursing; then He says it's OK to go, but He is furious when Balaam climbs on his donkey and actually starts out. Finally God says, OK, go, but the words you speak will be Mine. Is Balaam a con man or a true prophet? Some rabbis considered him the real thing, but most consider him to be wicked, in the same light as Amalek and Haman. He had no love for Israel. Left to his own devices, he would happily have cursed the Israelites and collected his reward from Balak.

There are several themes in today's *Parasha*. One, according to Alter, pivots on the act of *seeing*. Balaam refers to himself as "a man open-eyed—who beholds the vision of God, with eyes unveiled." Yet he can't see as well as his poor, mistreated donkey. He surrounds each attempt at cursing with great visual ceremony: seven altars are created. For each, seven bulls and seven rams will be sacrificed. This scene is repeated three times—all these numbers are rich in biblical significance. This theatrical production is intended to awe and impress the eyes of Balak and his followers. Further, in order to curse the Israelites, Balaam has to be able to see the enemy he intends to harm.

The act of seeing, of going beyond looking, is a frequent theme in Torah; it calls us to look beyond superficialities to see what *is*, what's before us, and also what can be; opening our eyes to the real world, absorbing its beauty, but also directing us to the places where there is work to be done to complete God's creation. The Torah calls us to recognize injustice, suffering, and poverty—with eyes wide open so that we can fulfill our obligation to repair the world. And even when engaging with the Torah itself, the rabbis have taught us to go deeper than the written words, probing their meaning, probing even the white spaces between the words. It is this tradition, I think, that has turned us into a people rich with philosophers, scientists, writers, artists, skeptics: Einstein and Mel Brooks; Freud and Jerry Seinfeld.

A second theme pivots around the power of speech. When Balak first becomes fearful of Moses and the Israelites, he seeks out the Midianites to discover the secret of Moses' power. After all, Moses lived among the Midianites, was counseled by Jethro, a Midianite priest, married Jethro's daughter. They know him.

"Where does this Moses get his power?" Balak asks.

"Only from his mouth," he is told.

How extraordinary. Moses, who protested to God that he can't speak with Pharaoh because his mouth is impaired, uncircumcised, is credited by Balak with having magical powers of speech. And so Balak decides to vanquish Moses and the Israelites by recruiting still another mouth—not the mouth of the donkey, though that might have been a better choice, but of Balaam: "Those whom you bless are truly blessed," Balak says, "and those whom you curse are cursed." Come, I will reward you to curse the Israelites.

In his commentary on the *Parasha*, Alter indicates that the essential lesson of Balak is that any attempt to alter history through magical incantations is futile. Only God controls human destiny. But that doesn't mean that words have no power over people or events. We know that God takes spoken words seriously. "Do not take the Lord's name in vain," the third Commandment instructs us. Be careful what you vow, because vows are binding, not to be treated lightly. *Lashon hara, evil speech,* is a serious sin, the rabbis teach us, comparable to murder or idol worship. Even our beloved Miriam is chastised by God for speaking against Moses.

Words are powerful. They inflame or they comfort. They enrage or they inspire. They can change the course of history, not through magic, but by influencing others to think and act in certain ways. At the close of the Civil War, Lincoln used elegant words to start the process of healing and reconciliation: "With malice towards none; with charity for all …"

During the dark days of World War II, Churchill and Roosevelt took to the airways to lift our spirits. "The only thing we have to fear is fear itself," Roosevelt said. Across the country we gathered in our living rooms, staring at a blank, inert radio, and those words gave us hope and courage.

Words have also been spoken with evil intent. Hitler was a masterful orator who galvanized a nation to unthinkable destruction and cruelty. Korah tried to undermine Moses and Aaron through flattery and deceit. The spies that Moses sent out to reconnoiter the land spoke words that doomed the Israelites to wander the desert for forty years until their generation all perished.

Gossip can surely affect a person's life. The midrash has it that the second Temple was destroyed because of wanton gossip. In our own time, the bullying that occurs on social media is a powerful example of how terribly a young person can be affected by the mockery of his or her peers, even to the point of suicide.

Words are powerful, but they are not magical; they do not disrupt the laws of nature. Those powers are reserved for God. The prayers we say do not cause the Twins to win, any more than the curses flung at our boys by the other fans cause them to lose. It's that hanging curve ball that did it.

We pray for understanding, for forgiveness, for rain in its season, for healing when we or those we love are afflicted, but mostly, I think, for the strength to carry on, and for the comfort of family and friends in our times of trouble. And sometimes the most useful, comforting words are the ones not spoken. When our daughter, Karen, died, my friend Chuck said, "There are no words…" and that was enough, and all too true.

Balaam climbed upon his ass and set out to curse a people chosen by God to be a nation of priests. It made no difference what Balaam would have said had God allowed him to speak his mind. God's plan for us didn't require Balaam's blessings and would not have been altered by his curses. Our destiny was carved in stone, on tablets, and not on the tongue of Balaam or any other villain who wishes us ill. Balaam's ass was wise. It didn't speak until the occasion required it—until it became necessary to bring this foolish man to his senses. And then it said just what was necessary. There is no record of any other speech or dvar Torah given by the donkey.

Ultimately, Balaam gave us a timeless gift. He spoke rapturously about our people and his words have entered and enriched our liturgy. We learn later that Balaam died a violent death, but not until he had attempted serious mischief that threatened the Jewish people just as we were about to enter Canaan. Only quick action by Pinchus averted God's anger and saved us. We know that Balaam did not wish us well, but we ignore the messenger and embrace the message. May that message, that ancient blessing, always hold true: in God's eyes, in the eyes of the world, and, no less important, in our own: *Ma tovu ohalekha Yaakov, mishknotekha Yisrael—how goodly are your tents, O Jacob, your dwellings, O Israel.*

Shabbat Shalom!

# Va'etchanan
## (Deuteronomy 3:23-7:11)

TODAY'S *PARASHA* OPENS WITH one of the most poignant episodes in the Torah. God has told Moses that soon he will die and that he will not be with the people when they enter the Promised Land. His most cherished wish has been denied.

For more than forty years, Moses has devoted his whole existence, his personal life, his family life, to the will of God. The things most of us crave—comfort, love, a peaceful old age—all of these he gave up to serve God. And now he pleads unsuccessfully to see his Mission Accomplished. He is beseeching God not for riches, not for personal gain, not for an inheritance for his children. He asks only for the chance to place a foot on the hallowed soil of the Promised Land. I know that many in this sanctuary have been to Israel. Think of it. We have had a privilege denied to our greatest prophet.

It is hard to imagine that God could refuse him. And yet, what Moses experiences is not unknown to us. We share his fate. None of us quite goes over into the good land, the place where our children and grandchildren will dwell. We've worked so hard, worried so much about their welfare, we want to see how their journey proceeds, how they make their way in the world. We want to be there to help, to guide, but it cannot be. Our lives are beginnings and preparations for works that others will have to complete. We marry and have children. We open a door for them, and they leave us behind. They set out on new journeys with new companions. We witness from a distance, waving anxiously and proudly, but we can't go along. Like Moses on the other side of the Jordan, we glimpse, but we don't enter that good land.

Moses lived a life of unexpected turns and twists, and he himself is full of contradictions. He starts out as a basket case, but becomes a prince of Egypt. From that exalted station, he is soon reduced to a fugitive, fleeing for his life into the desert. He sheds his royal clothes and becomes a common shepherd. From the moment he encounters God in the burning bush, his life will be entirely devoted to his own people, and yet he marries an outsider, the daughter of Jethro, a Midianite priest.

He is father to the Israelite nation, but no father to his own children. In one of the strangest episodes in the Torah, he is almost killed for failing to circumcise his son. According to *Midrash*, he was more attentive to Aaron's sons than to his own. His children don't enter the family business. They do not become prophets or inspired leaders. They are mentioned briefly, and then disappear from the Torah. We know that Moses is a just and humble man, but he is quick to anger, and needs the restraining influence of Aaron and Miriam. He leads with fierce authority and is respected and feared, but he is not loved. That is another sacrifice he makes in the service of the grumbling, stiff-necked Israelites.

When God first called Moses to lead the Jews out of Egypt, he resisted: "Please, O Lord, I have never been a man of words, either in times past or now that You have spoken to Your servant; I am slow of speech and slow of tongue (Exodus 4:10)." Moses hesitates to approach Pharaoh because he is a stutterer. God assures Moses that He will be with him and will tell Moses what to say, but still Moses pleads with God. "Please, O Lord, make someone else your agent." God strikes a compromise. He will speak to Moses, Moses will speak to Aaron, and Aaron will deliver God's message. This is the first recorded version of the old "telephone" game.

Moses finally agrees. He and Aaron assemble the elders of Israel. Aaron—not Moses— repeats God's words and performs the wondrous signs in sight of the people. Next Moses and Aaron go to Pharaoh and present God's demand: "Let my children go!" At first, Aaron does all the talking, but as each of the plagues is announced, Moses gradually takes over. In the last four plagues, Moses performs the signs and wonders, not Aaron. From this point on, Moses grows in authority. He no longer complains about his slowness of speech and he no longer asks Aaron to speak for him.

I spent forty years as a professor of speech pathology, and I lectured and did research in stuttering. If you've seen the movie *The King's Speech*, you have a pretty good idea how devastating stuttering can be. It is understandable that Moses would resist a leadership position in which he must speak for God. There are two questions that jump out for anyone who has studied the problem of stuttering. First, how did Moses become a stutterer, and second, how did he overcome his stuttering?

The Midrash has an answer for the first question. In the Midrash, when young Moses was in Pharaoh's court, his advisors suspected that he was no ordinary child and feared that he might try to usurp the throne, so they arranged a test. Moses was placed in front of hot glowing coals on one side, and sparkling jewels on the other. Moses was about to reach for the precious stones but an angel guided his hand to the coals. Moses put his inflamed hand in his mouth and burned his lips and tongue. He survived the burns, but he became "slow of speech."

We learn from this Midrash that God was looking out for Moses. He assigned an angel full-time to his care. We also learn that the rabbis explained Moses' stuttering by something external, something that happened to him—burning fingers that scarred his mouth. My father stuttered and he agreed with the rabbis. The reason he gave was that he had swallowed lye when he was a child. Most stutterers today didn't swallow lye or burn their tongues, and despite the sages and the ages, the cause of stuttering is still a mystery.

But why did the rabbis think it important to explain the origins of Moses' stuttering? Perhaps they were uncomfortable with the idea that God had chosen an imperfect vessel to be His *shaliach*, His messenger. The stuttering had to have come about from some external event, certainly not from God. In this, I believe there is more wisdom in the Torah than in the Midrash. When Moses tries to shirk his duty, pleading his speech impediment, God rather impatiently says: "Who gives man speech? Who makes him dumb or deaf, seeing or blind? Is it not I, the Lord?" (Exodus 4:11). I think God is saying to Moses: You stutter? So what. I've got a job for you to do.

The Torah doesn't tell us how Moses was cured of his stuttering, though according to R. Joshua Ben Levi (cited by Aviva Zornberg), Moses was healed when he "came to merit the Torah." One old joke is that God told him to take two tablets and call in the morning. Many stutterers would be more than willing to climb a mountain, fast for forty days, throw themselves into a burning bush—if only it cured them. However, God was not concerned with Moses' speech problem. God arranged to have Aaron talk for Moses only because Moses insisted. If God had wanted to "cure" Moses, He surely could have. Perhaps Moses never was "cured," but in the end it didn't matter. His stuttering did not become a "handicap." That's what the blind and the deaf and the physically challenged in our community insist on. They don't want to be considered handicapped. They can cope. They can succeed. They only need a fair opportunity.

We learn from Moses' experience that we don't have to be perfect to do important work. King George VI was called on to inspire his people despite his lifelong struggle with stuttering. Moses was chosen by God despite his own insistence that he was not fit. In a tradition such as ours that reveres the spoken word, it is thrilling that God chose Moses, a stutterer, to lead His people.

I mentioned earlier that my father, Abraham Gershom, stuttered. He also coped with painful anxieties throughout his adult life. Still, he worked, sometimes two jobs, he raised two sons, both of whom raised Jewish children of their own, he was a Cub Scout leader and president of his synagogue Men's Club.

We are all limited in some way. But there are always people who need our comfort and help. There are always important, constructive tasks to begin even if they are not completed in our own time. For each of us there is a burning bush calling us to service, not so grand as leading a nation across a wilderness, but no less important for the survival of our people and of the world. Perhaps we will not hear God's fearsome voice in thunder and lightning, but if we listen with our hearts, we will hear a still, small voice urging us to devote our talents, with all our imperfections, to tikkun olam, not only to walk in places that are holy, but also to make holy the places where we walk. This too we find in today's Torah reading.

Shabbat Shalom!

# Ekev
## (Deuteronomy 7:12—11:25)

IN TODAY'S TORAH PORTION, the Israelites are about to enter the Promised Land where many battles have yet to be fought and the enemies of Israel have to be vanquished. But even when external enemies are defeated, we struggle with the enemy within. Who was it, after all, that Jacob wrestled with, alone in the desert, before he was blessed and given the name Israel? Jacob needed to confront and overcome his inner demons. The greatest threat to the Israelites was not the Canaanites. God took care of them. The most enduring challenge has always been to tame the *yetzer harah*, our own uncharitable and destructive impulses. I grew up with a comic strip called *Pogo*, written by Walt Kelly. Pogo summarized a good part of Deuteronomy when he said, "We have met the enemy, and he is us."

There is a popular saying that in life the journey is more important than reaching a destination. For forty years the Israelites trekked across the unforgiving desert, dependent on God for food and water, for direction, for survival. A whole generation had to die in the desert. Even our greatest leaders, Miriam, Aaron, and Moses, did not cross over to the Promised Land. The Midrash tells us that Moses pleaded with God to enter the land in any shape or form, but he was denied. For him, there was only the journey.

For the Jewish people, the real journey—the one we are still on—didn't end when we took possession of Canaan. Rather, that was the real beginning of our eternal journey—our obligation to pursue justice, charity, loving-kindness, to care for the weak and the stranger; to make our daily lives holy. Once we entered the Promised Land, a new, spiritual journey began, and responsibility for tikkun olam, repair of the world, became ours.

We are no longer a rag-tag group of former slaves plodding across the desert to an unknown destination. God no longer gives us manna, but there are still people who are hungry. God no longer provides clothing that won't wear out, but there are people who are cold and homeless. We no longer have God's global positioning system to guide us—the fire at night and the clouds during the day—but we still have to find our way. Rav Nachman of Breslau told that his grandfather, the Baal Shem Tov, used to go to a certain place in the woods, build a fire, and utter a special prayer to bring God's blessing to the suffering people. After he died, his disciples no longer knew the place, but they still could light the fire and say the prayer. The next generations didn't recall how to create the fire, and then, eventually, they also forgot the words. But they were not entirely bereft, because they still had the story of the place and the fire and the words.

Early in our history, we tried to reach heaven by erecting a high tower. We have since learned that heaven will find us if we are partners with God in building shelters of peace. We were liberated from slavery. We know the difference between good and evil. We were granted free will. With these gifts came the responsibility to follow paths of righteousness even though we no longer have the cloud and the fire to guide us. Like the Baal Shem's students, we are not bereft and we are not abandoned. We have the story of how it was done. We have the Torah and the wisdom of our sages, and our own devoted teachers who are eager to join us in new journeys of learning and understanding to help us discover paths of righteousness—Ekev—to follow in God's footsteps.

This day is special for me in several respects. I couldn't think of a present that I could give to my wife, Eileen, on this, our fiftieth anniversary, that would adequately express my appreciation and love, and so this sermon is for her. And just two years ago I was scheduled to give a d'var Torah during the summer months, but I couldn't because of the loss of our beloved daughter, Karen. The portion, as it turns out, was to be *Parasha* Ekev.

Shabbat Shalom!

# Ki Tetze
(Deuteronomy 21:10–25:19)

AT THE VERY END of today's Torah reading, when the Israelites are finally poised to enter the Promised Land after forty years in the desert, Moses tells them: Remember what Amalek did to you on the way when you came out of Egypt, how he fell upon you on the way and cut down all the stragglers, with you famished and exhausted, and he did not fear God (Deuteronomy 25: 17-18).

There is a lot packed into that sentence. When I first read it, I thought only about the treachery done by Amalek, but Moses is also reminding the Israelites how much their parents, that first generation who followed Moses out of Egypt and into the unknown, suffered on the way to the Promised Land that they never got to enter. I was struck by that because the Torah is not often sympathetic to that first generation of complaining, stiff-necked former slaves.

The very next sentence in our *Parasha* seems totally enigmatic, and perhaps that's why I find it so fascinating: You shall wipe out the remembrance of Amalek from under the heavens, you shall not forget (Deuteronomy, 25:19).

That reminds me of one of those Zen Buddhist mystical sayings: What is the sound of one hand clapping? (In my family it was one hand "*klopping*," not clapping, usually my mother's hand on some part of my lower anatomy.) By telling us not to forget to *wipe out the remembrance of Amalek from under the heavens,* God has guaranteed that the name of Amalek will never be wiped out. How can it be when it is written in the Torah? Here we are reading and studying and talking about Amalek thousands of years later.

In Exodus (17:14), God declares that He will do the job for us. He will "wipe out the name of Amalek under the heavens," but later Moses tells the Israelites: "The Lord will have war with Amalek from generation to generation" (Exodus, 17:16). Again, these statements seem contradictory. If God intends to wipe out Amalek, why will He still be at war with Amalek across the generations?

If the Amalekites are with us in our generation, I wonder what we're supposed to do with them. How to respond to the Amalekites is not an esoteric question. In 1994 when Baruch Goldstein opened fire on Muslim worshippers at the Tomb of the Patriarchs in Hebron, I suspect he felt he was doing a mitzvah, destroying modern-day Amalek.

And in 2006, Rabbi Jack Reimer, a distinguished Conservative rabbi, wrote: "I am slowly but surely and reluctantly becoming convinced that we of the western world are confronting the kind of evil that Amalek represents. I am becoming convinced that Islamic Fundamentalism, or, as some people prefer to call it, Islamo-fascism, is the most dangerous force that we have ever faced and that it is worthy of the name: Amalek… We must recognize who Amalek is in our generation, and we must prepare to fight it in every way we can. And may God help us in this task." (Weekly Torah commentary on *Parasha B'shallah*.)

Rabbi Reimer's remarks are troubling. If we convince ourselves that our enemies are Amalekites, we give ourselves the authority, even the obligation, of Torah, to destroy them—men, women, children. Using the Torah in that way can be dangerous. One of the lessons our *Parasha* teaches is that having reverence for the Torah means we have to acknowledge and live with its contradictions. Having faith in the Torah does not mean that we unthinkingly use it to resolve every conflict or ethical or moral problem. Instead, the Torah itself includes narratives that challenge our ethical and moral principles and force us to confront them. Is Abraham's response in the *Akeda* an example of true faith? Would we be willing to sacrifice a child if God commanded it? Does faith require us to carry out a Torah command when it feels unjust?

I think that some of what appear to be statements in the Torah are best understood as questions. For example, when I read: blot out the memory of Amalek, I translate that declarative sentence into a set of questions: Does God truly wish us to destroy an entire people? Doesn't that feel like genocide? What if there are ten righteous men or women among them? How literally should we understand those words? What is the moral way to deal with historic adversaries? How can we reconcile these chilling words with the compassion and justice that are the principal messages of Torah?

May we express consternation with the Torah when it describes harsh punishment like the command to stone to death a rebellious son or a Sabbath violator, or to wipe out an entire community? If we accept everything in Torah unquestioningly, we miss important teaching and learning opportunities. We need to compare the words of any particular section of Torah with the Torah in its entirety. If something in our judgment doesn't fit, violates the spirit of the Torah, we need to acknowledge that. If we don't question the Torah, we treat it as a relic rather than a living doctrine.

Dare we find fault with decisions that God has made? That sounds heretical, except that such questioning is an intrinsic part of our heritage. On numerous occasions Moses expresses disapproval of God's decisions, and God relents and changes a decree. Throughout the ages our rabbis and sages have honored God by passionately arguing with Him. Rabbi Yitzchok of Berdichev famously confronts God: "Dear Riboyno Shel Oylem (Master of the Universe), I will not move from this spot until you take pity on your suffering people."

I would add: Dear Riboyno Shel Oylem, we cannot carry out Your command to stone the rebellious child, or ostracize the misbegotten, or turn away from the anguish of the abandoned wife, or banish the physically impaired, because that is not Your way, because Your Torah teaches us to be just and merciful and these commands are neither just nor merciful!

The Torah provides lessons, not recipes. It is a not an instruction book with unambiguous, clear, settled directions about how to live one's life as a Jew. Pinchas received God's blessing for killing an Israelite who was sinning in a public place. That does not mean that I have permission to do the same. The Torah does not spell out when zealotry in the service of God is a mitzvah, and when it is a travesty in God's eyes. I don't believe that anyone can consult the Torah to determine who the Amalekites are in our modern world so that we may obliterate them with confidence that we are carrying out God's intention.

To have faith in the Torah does not mean blind faith. The Torah encourages us to think, question, explore, argue. Moses received the Torah, but that was only a beginning. Receiving the Torah is like receiving a highly useful tool in a beautifully wrapped package. We can become so taken with the beauty of the package that we are reluctant to open it. Or we can carefully unwrap the tool and then place it on a mantle to be admired alongside the photograph of our favorite aunt and uncle. But if we want it to make a difference in our lives, it has to be unpacked, handled, used. That is the essence of our tradition. We are not to admire the Torah from afar. We need to dig in and turn it over and over so that we can be turned. We are told that the Israelites when offered the Torah said: We will do and we will understand, and that is taken as an expression of great faith. But I think the two should go hand in hand, or the doing will be meaningless and rote. I believe that doing without understanding is one reason we have Jews who excel in ritual but fail utterly to live a Torah life.

The words in our *Parasha* are just the doorway to a vast landscape of knowledge, understanding, and wisdom. The Torah invites us to enter, stumble around, try different paths, different interpretations, always striving to become even more lost, to go deeper and deeper into it. Reading the Torah in this manner takes courage and humility. It means that we acknowledge that we do not understand with perfect clarity what God wishes of us. And it means we forage in territory that is forever new, even though we've been there many times before. And if there is blotting out to be done, may it be of ignorance, prejudice, poverty, and hatred.

Shabbat Shalom!

# Re'eh
## (Deuteronomy 11:26-16:17)

TODAY'S *PARASHA* BEGINS WITH the words: "See, I place before you a blessing and a curse…." *You* in that verse is in the plural, referring to the entire community. Standard English doesn't distinguish between singular "you" and plural "you," but Hebrew does, and so does the dialect I grew up with. In Brooklyn, we would say, "See, I place before *youse* a blessing and a curse." That ain't grammatical English, but it gets the job done. What that plural *you* means is that we are responsible for each other. We celebrate with each other, we mourn with each other, and our destiny as well as our history is intertwined.

I am puzzled by the very first word in today's reading: Re'eh—"*See.*"

Picture the scene. Moses was admonishing the people, summarizing their experiences over the last forty years, telling them what God wants of them and how they are to flourish in the new land God is giving them. But what was there to see? Moses didn't have a slide show or a PowerPoint presentation. The lessons of Torah were presented orally—Shma Yisroel—Hear O Israel. Why *See*? I don't think Moses was calling attention to himself. *See, it's me, Moses, up on this hill, talking to you.* That would have been out of character. The Torah tells us that Moses was a most humble man.

The Torah doesn't waste words. There must be a reason our *Parasha* begins as it does. I think the Torah wants us to understand that see means more than *look*. In this context, *see* means that we should take what we see and search for its meaning—even more, we should strive to give it meaning. That's how we truly learn Torah. It's an active process that involves the brain and the heart, not a passive one of letting the eyeballs do all the work.

I have a friend whose passion is bird-watching. Sometimes I am with him and he says, "Look, look, there's an orange-winged, green-tufted, short-beaked Shomer Shabbos Yarmulke bird." I look and, on a good day, I can maybe make out a rustle of leaves in the tree he is pointing to, but that's it. I look, but I don't see.

The Torah is always asking us to see more than is obvious. In this same *Parasha* Moses warns the people: Any prophet who invites you to worship other gods is false, even if he performs miracles, or correctly prophesies the future. The lesson is: Don't be taken in by illusions, by magic, by spectacles, by con men. Don't be deluded by appearances. See what is true and holy.

There are other examples in Torah where we learn that looking is not the same as seeing. Abraham has brought his beloved son to Mount Moriah, and Isaac, the silent one, asks: "Father, where is the animal that we are to sacrifice?" Abraham says, "God will provide," but, paradoxically, Abraham is unable to see God's true nature. He is just about to sacrifice his son when the angel calls to him. Then Abraham lifts his eyes and sees the ram that was there all the time— that was there from the beginning of time. How could Abraham have thought that God would wish him to offer his son as a sacrifice? In fact, in today's *Parasha*, God says to the Israelites: You are not to follow the ways of the people you are about to dispossess, for their practices are an abomination—they are willing to sacrifice their own children. (12:31) Their ways are not our ways. God does not ask us to sacrifice our children. Sometimes faith and devotion can obscure our vision.

Isaac survives that ordeal, but his eyes grow dim and he is tricked into giving his blessing to Jacob rather than Esau. Jacob's deceit is troubling, but I wonder why Isaac couldn't see that Jacob rather than Esau was destined to fulfill the covenant. Like Esau, Isaac's appetite for food interferes with his vision. As I read the text, however, it seems to me that perhaps he is not really duped—that he is willing to be deceived, perhaps because in that way he can carry out God's plan, and still get a solid meal from each of his sons.

Balaam is riding an ass on his way to curse the Israelites, and the ass sees an angel blocking the way; but Balaam does not. He is blinded by his greed, by his evil inclination, and the ass makes an ass out of Balaam.

Moses sends twelve spies to scout out Canaan—the promised land—and ten report only what *is*, and not what *can be*, and because of their inability to see beyond their eyes, they and all their generation except for Caleb and Joshua die in the desert.

Jacob rests his head on a rock, and only when he has closed his eyes does he see angels ascending and descending the ladder. But then his eyes are opened and he knows he is in God's presence. For that recognition alone he is worthy of becoming Israel, and we his inheritance.

In today's *Parasha*, Moses makes two statements that seem contradictory. He says: There will not be among you any needy person, for God will bless you in the land that your God is giving you. (15:2). But just a few verses later he says: The needy will never be gone from amid the land (15:11). How can both of these statements be true? The first is the ideal—a world as we would like it to be, where there are no poor; and the second is the reality, the world as it is. It is important not to wear blinders, to see the world as it is, but also to have a vision of how it might be. We devise means to protect ourselves from seeing the needy; we contrive to hide them from our view, but the Torah teaches us that we must see beyond our own circumstances and reach out to those in need.

Moses tells the Israelites that God will select a site where they can worship and sacrifice, and that God will place His name there. Not God Himself, but His name. God's name is not visible. We need another kind of vision to see God—the vision that comes from continual questioning and study.

We see God through His works and through our own yearnings. We are constantly recreating God in our own image, but that image has been shaped by Torah. I think that today's *Parasha* is telling us: Don't just look, but *see*. See the needy in our midst; see the injustice in the world; see the opportunities for deeds of loving kindness; see what is possible as well as what is, but don't confuse the two; see the goodness in ourselves and one another. And if, like Isaac, our eyes are dim, the Torah is there to help us find our way through a world that is often chaotic and confusing.

Shabbat Shalom!

# Ki Tavo
(Deuteronomy 26:1-29:8).

THIS DAY HAS SPECIAL resonance for me because exactly one hundred and two years ago, my mother, Naomi Needleman Siegel, was born in New York City, and just last Monday we observed her yahrzeit. And so, I dedicate this Torah study to her memory and from time to time I will bring her into the conversation.

We are coming to the end of Deuteronomy, the last book of the Torah, and soon we will observe the High Holy Days and start the Torah cycle again. In Deuteronomy, Moses takes center stage and he delivers a long and majestic monologue. Ki Tavo, today's *Parasha*, is part of the second discourse that is the core of Deuteronomy, with Moses reviewing the laws he received from God at Mount Sinai. The Israelites are finally about to enter Canaan. We know, and Moses knows, that soon after his last words are spoken, his life will end. But first he will write out the book we know of as Deuteronomy, and have it placed beside the Ark of the Covenant.

Ki Tavo is a treasure house of thought-provoking material, but there are two themes that especially caught my attention. The Torah tells us that it was in the fortieth year, on the first day of the eleventh month, that Moses addressed the Israelites (Deuteronomy1:3). Starting on that day he gave five long speeches, or discourses. In today's *Parasha*, Moses repeatedly uses the words, "this day" or "today." For example:

"*This day* the Lord your God charges you to do these statutes and these laws …." (Deuteronomy 26:16).

"The Lord you have proclaimed *this day* to be your God… (26:17)."

"The Lord has proclaimed you *this day* to be to Him a treasured people…" (26:18).

"Moses… spoke to all Israel, saying, 'Be still and listen, Israel. *This day* you have become a people to the Lord your God.'" (27:9).

In these and other examples, the Torah mentions a particular day. I feel sure, however, that these references are intended to be timeless. Moses is speaking not only to the assembled Israelites, but to us as well. Today, when we and every other Jewish congregation read the verses that Moses spoke—this is the day when we and God choose each other in covenant. Every day we are given the opportunity to reaffirm the covenant. Every day is the day to engage in acts of loving-kindness; every day we can learn more about our tradition, our history, and the gifts our tradition has offered to the betterment of humankind.

My mother, who was born more than 100 years ago today, would not allow the hospital to bill Medicare for services she did not receive, even though it would cost her nothing. She would not remain in the apartment she had lived in for fifty years when her landlord threatened to evict a young couple with a baby because my mother's apartment was rent-controlled and theirs was not. And she would not allow age and infirmity to prevent her from voting in a presidential election—a determination, or stubbornness, that was rewarded with a fall and a broken arm. By recalling these things now, *those* days become *this* day. So it is with the Torah. If the Torah is truly an *Etz Haim*, a Tree of Life, it must be a living tree, and like any living thing, it needs to be nourished. As we study and engage with Torah, we provide that nourishment and keep it alive so that we can cling to it and live within its shelter.

At the very end of Ki Tavo, Moses spoke words to the Israelites that puzzle me: You have seen all that the Lord did before your own eyes in the Land of Egypt…the great trials that your own eyes have seen, those great signs and portents. But the Lord has not given you a heart to understand and eyes to see and ears to hear until this day (29:1-4).

It is the last part of that verse that gives me pause: *God has not given you a heart to understand, eyes to see, and ears to hear.*

If God didn't give the Israelites a heart to understand, how can they be held accountable for their failures of understanding? On a personal level, if I accept a bribe, or give false witness, or cheat in business, may I say in my defense, "It's because God didn't give me a heart to understand?" Or, if I avert my eyes from a person in need, or turn a deaf ear to the cry of the orphan, may I claim: "It's because God didn't give me eyes to see or ears to hear"? I don't think that is what the Torah demands of us. We may not shift the blame to God for our personal failures. So, where do seeing, hearing, understanding come from, if not directly from God?

In Nitzavim, the Torah portion we will be reading next Shabbos, Moses gives good news to the assembled Israelites. He tells them that God will open their hearts. That sounds like God is doing all the "heart" work. God will pry open their hearts. But that's not quite how it will happen. First the Israelites will stray from the path of righteousness and will suffer the awful curses that we read about in today's *Parasha.* When they return and follow the commandments, *with all their heart and soul,* as it is written, God will then take them back with love, and will then open their hearts to love God. God plays a part in this quickening of devotion, but only when we have met certain conditions, when we already have love in our heart and soul.

Another example. In the Book of Daniel we read: God gives wisdom to the wise and knowledge to those who have understanding (Dan. 2:29-23). The logic seems twisted. If one is already wise and understanding, what does it mean that God gives wisdom and knowledge? I think the point is that these gifts are conditional. We make ourselves accessible to them by preparing to receive them.

One last example. Balaam is riding on a donkey on his way to curse the Israelites and does not see the angel blocking the donkey's way. We recognize the irony of this passage. The donkey is more aware of God's presence than this prophet, this so-called seer. The text tells us that God opens Balaam's eyes and he finally sees the angel. Balaam's blindness did not come from God. His own greed blinded him. Balaam did not have eyes to see the goodness of Israel or a heart to understand that they were on a sacred mission because he had closed his heart and filled it with malice.

These examples teach us that knowledge, understanding, wisdom, insight—all these desirable attributes—are not outright gifts. We may ask God to turn us to righteousness, as we do in many of our prayers, but those prayers are empty unless we first turn ourselves. God gives understanding to those who are open to understanding. On the other hand, if our hearts are closed, God will not open them, perhaps cannot open them. In Exodus we read that God "hardened Pharaoh's heart," but Pharaoh's heart was already hard and cruel long before his encounter with Moses.

*Ki Tavo*, "When you come in…" In today's *Parasha*, that means when you come in to the Land. I would suggest it also means that when we *come in to Torah*, we will find eyes to see, ears to hear, and a heart to understand how to make a more just, peaceful, and loving world.

Finally, I want to close with a short tribute to my mother. My Tante Chaika and my grandmother competed to do the fancy baking and holiday cooking in our family—*varnishkes, verenikes, rugelekh, mandl broyt, helzl, gefilte fish, grivenes, borscht*. But my mother did have one special dish that she made every Passover when she visited us. It's a dish with sour prunes that she brought with her from Brooklyn, stuffed with walnuts. To these she added glazed orange and lemon slices; a glistening, sweet, and sticky concoction. Guests at our family seders were enthusiastic with their praise.

This last Pesach, Shmuel Shulman wrote to tell me that once again he prepared "Mrs. Naomi Siegel's Walnut Filled Prunes" for his seder in Israel. My mother has been gone for eight years, but her recipe lives on; she has an international following. The recipe is on the very last page of *L'Dor V'Dor*, the *Adath Women's League Cook Book*. I submitted it in her name. Sharing my mother's recipe with this community, bringing her into this community, gives me great pleasure. May her memory be for a blessing. And may we all be blessed with sweet memories as we approach the New Year.

Shabbat Shalom!

# Nitzavim
## (Deuteronomy 29:9–30:20)

I WANT TO FOCUS on one passage in *Parasha* Nitzavim, really just a few words. The section is Deuteronomy 29:24-28. The statement in Hertz's translation is: "The secret things belong unto the Lord our God; but the things that are revealed belong unto us and our children forever, that we may do all the words of this law."

I wondered what these "secret things" might be, why they belong to God, and what we are supposed to do about them—if anything. If they belong to God, that might mean that they are forbidden to us. But secrets are tantalizing, so maybe God intended to capture our curiosity with these secrets and to entice us to search for their meaning.

There is something puzzling even about how this passage is transcribed in the Torah. Several of the Hebrew words have tiny dots over them. The words with the dots are translated as, "to us and our children forever." The commentary tells us that this is one of fifteen verses in all of the Bible which have these dots. The dots appear in the Torah scrolls and in any Hebrew volume that faithfully reproduces the Torah. The dots do not appear in the English translation.

Nothing in the Torah is superfluous, and so the rabbis have attempted to determine what these dots might mean. There are differing opinions. Hertz suggests that the dots are intended to call attention to particularly important words. However there are many other equally important clusters of words that don't have dots over them.

Plaut posits that the dots hint at a "concealed meaning" in the highlighted words. But we have already learned that concealed or secret things belong to God, and here we are searching for the meaning of the dots. Are we violating a law by trying to understand their presence? If the meanings belong only to God, why do they appear so conspicuously in the Torah? The way our minds work, we are drawn to them like a magnet.

Maybe it is wrong to assume that because something belongs to God, it belongs *only* to God. Maybe God intends to share His secrets. The universe is full of secrets. The human mind is a secret. The miracles of birth and death are secret. Just recently my mother died and as I saw the incomprehensible transition between being alive and being dead, I realized I had just witnessed a great and mysterious secret that surely belongs to God. But these secrets are invitations to explore, question, seek knowledge and understanding. As I studied these few lines of text, it seemed to me that human progress is a constant attempt to penetrate God's secrets. Yes, the secret things belong to God, but not exclusively. God fashioned us in such a way that it is our destiny to probe these secrets; they are irresistible.

That's why I don't hold a grudge against Adam and Eve. There they were in the Garden of Eden, looking at *the tree of the knowing of good and evil,* in Fox's translation, and the snake said, if you eat from that tree your eyes will be opened and you will become like gods, knowing good and evil (Genesis 3:5). Of course they defied God. God must have known they would, or why put the tree there in the first place? Knowledge is irresistible to us. Adam and Eve had to partake of the tree of knowledge. What would human existence be if there was no knowledge of the difference between good and evil? In the Torah we are constantly exhorted to choose between blessings and curses, between moral and immoral behavior, between good and evil, the very knowledge for which Adam and Eve forfeited their place in the time-share known as the Garden of Eden.

I don't think of Adam and Eve as having sinned. They did just what humans are supposed to do—in current vernacular, what we are programmed to do. They were curious, and that got them into trouble, but it is our nature to be curious. God has given us the capacity to reason and has endowed us with the will to learn. If I had been around when those guys were erecting a large tower in the town of

Babel, I might just have pitched in. They were reaching for heaven. They were searching for knowledge of God, as were Adam and Eve, and Moses, who asked to see God, to know God's name.

We no longer have the tree of knowledge in our backyard, and the difference between good and evil is not always so clearly drawn. We know that they exist, but we do not always know which is which. We have no choice. We are compelled to explore and to learn. So we study. We study Torah, and we study the physical world God created. He filled us with the capacity to create science, philosophy, and religion—to give a moral and ethical context for our knowledge.

The secret things belong to God, but I don't think that God intends that these things be secret forever. As we study Torah, we ask, "What does God want of us?" And as we pose that question, some of the secret things become ours and our children's. When we participate in and contribute to all of the education programs sponsored by our synagogues and our community, we help make the secret things revealed, so that they will "belong unto us and our children forever, that we may do all the words of this law." As we go out from this service, I hope we will have a reverence for study and knowledge, and will understand God's secrets as invitations and not barriers.

Shabbat Shalom!

# The Children's Corner

# The Most Famous Man in the World

THERE ONCE WAS AN ordinary man who lived with his wife and three children in an ordinary house. One day he decided that he didn't want to be ordinary anymore. He wanted to do something special so that he would be the Most Famous Man in the World.

He told his wife and children, "My dears, I must leave you for awhile. I have decided to become an artist. I'm going to paint a picture that is so beautiful that people will call me the Most Famous Artist in the World. Then you will be very proud of me and we will all be very happy."

His wife and children told him that they were already happy and they tried to persuade him to remain with them, but he wouldn't listen. He rented an artist's studio, where he placed an easel, canvas, and paints and brushes. He put an artist's beret on his head.

He said to himself, "I will paint a picture of all the things that people love to eat. That will be the most beautiful painting in the world because it will make people feel good in their stomachs as well as their eyes."

He painted pickles and peanut butter; applesauce and artichokes; cherries and chocolate ice cream; cotton candy and caramels; and much, much more.

When he was done he hung his painting in a gallery and many people came to look at it, but they all found something wrong with it. One person said, "This picture would be much better if you had included purple pomegranates and plump potato pancakes."

Some people complained that the peanut butter was too chunky, or that the applesauce was too tangy, or that dill pickles are better than sweet pickles, or that vanilla ice cream is better than chocolate.

One man held his stomach and groaned, "This picture is giving me a tummy ache."

So the man brought his painting back to his home. His wife and children were very glad to see him, but he was disappointed because he was no more famous than when he had left them.

At home he thought and thought about some other way to became famous. One day he told his family, "My dears, I'm going to leave you again. I've decided to write the most beautiful song that anyone has ever heard. When it's done, everyone will want to sing it and I will be the Most Famous Songwriter in the World. Then you'll be proud of me and we will all be very happy."

Once again his family tried to persuade him that they were already quite proud of him and wished he would stay home with them, but he wouldn't listen.

He went back to the studio and rented a piano so that he could compose his song. He said to himself, "My song will have all of the sounds that people love so that it will fill them with happiness when they hear it. It will have the sound of waves at the ocean; of an airplane bringing Grandma and Grandpa for a visit; of the first snowflakes of winter falling on a child's nose; of the rain stopping just before the Fourth of July parade; of packages being unwrapped at a birthday party; of fever coming down after an illness; and of being invited by a best friend to come out to play."

When it was done, he played the song at a concert. Many people came to hear it, but they all complained about something.

One man said, "You should have included the sound of butter brickle when it sticks to your teeth and you have to get it off with your tongue." He took out his false teeth and sure enough, there was butter brickle stuck in them.

A woman said, "You should have included the sound of bare feet squishing in the mud." She wasn't wearing shoes and you could tell she had been squishing that very day.

"Where are the birds? There should be bird songs," chirped one tall, skinny man who looked very much like a bird himself.

Some complained that the song was too loud, or too slow, or had too many sounds, or was too high, or low. The man who had a bellyache from the picture now held his head and said he had a headache from the song.

So, the man packed up his music and returned home, very discouraged because he was no more famous than when he had left. "I will never be famous," he said to himself.

When he opened the door to his house, he was greeted by his wife and children. He saw that his painting, nicely framed, was hanging on the wall. His song was on the piano and the children were playing it when he came in. They were all very glad to see him.

"Daddy, I'm so glad to see you," said one of the children. "Can you come to my dance recital tonight?"

And the other child said, "Daddy, tomorrow night I'm having a sleepover. Can you help move the furniture in my room?"

And the third child, who was too young to talk, just reached up to be held.

"You see," his wife said. "You are famous after all, to everyone in this house."

"And that's what's really important, isn't it?" said the man as he lifted his child high into the air.

"Yes," the two older children said, and the youngest just gurgled. "For us, you're the Most Famous Daddy in the World."

The man smiled. "You know," he said, "I'm very glad to be back home, but I'm also glad I went out into the world because it taught me a very important lesson."

"You should write what you learned in a story," his wife said.

"Do you think I could?" the man asked.

"Oh, of course," they all answered.

And so he did. This is the story he wrote.

# The King's Adviser

ONCE UPON A TIME there lived a king and queen who loved each other very much and were very happy except that the queen was neat and tidy but the king was very messy. The queen always placed her things just where they belonged, she never lost her crown or her eyeglasses, and never had a moustache, even after she drank chocolate milk. The king, however, didn't put his things back where they belonged and became quite grouchy when he couldn't find them. One morning he was especially grouchy.

"Where is my special pen? I can't sign a proclamation without my pen." He spoke very loudly.

"Your pen is just where you left it," the queen replied. "On your desk next to your peanut butter and jelly sandwich."

"Well, then," the king said, "where are my eyeglasses? I always keep them right here, next to my pen."

"My dear king," said the queen, "your eyeglasses are on your head, where you put them earlier this morning."

After the king misplaced his crown for the third or fourth time that morning, the queen decided, "This will never do. I can't be looking for the king's things all day long." She called for her page, Joshua Thumbkins.

She said, "I have a job for you. I want you to follow the king and note just where he leaves any of his things. Then, when the king is asleep, you must send your twenty-two children to gather up all of the king's belongings and put them in their proper place."

Joshua Thumbkins said, "Yes, Your Majesty," and he bowed so low that the tip of his nose touched the floor.

The next day when the king came to breakfast he said, "Something extraordinary has happened. When I awoke this morning all my things were exactly where they belong, and I don't remember putting them there. It feels wonderful to be so neat and tidy and know where everything is."

The queen smiled and said nothing about Joshua Thumbkins and his twenty-two children who were all snoring, exhausted, in their beds.

Later the queen called for Joshua Thumbkins. The poor man looked very haggard.

"How are you, Page Thumbkins?" she asked.

"A bit tired, Your Majesty, but I'll get used to it."

"And the children?"

"They are fine, Your Majesty, but keeping up with the king proved too much for them, and so we have asked their twenty-two Thumbkin cousins to help find and replace the King's belongings each night."

"Wonderful," said the queen. "Keep up the good work. The entire kingdom is grateful to you."

Joshua Thumbkins blushed at the compliment and he bowed so low his necktie became tangled with his shoelaces and he could not straighten up. He rolled and somersaulted out of the palace while the queen stared and stared.

From then on, when the king woke up he found everything exactly where it belonged and in its proper place. He never suspected how all of this happened. He began to think of himself as a very neat and tidy person and he decided that all of his subjects should follow his example. When he sat down to breakfast, he noticed that his pancakes were not perfectly round.

"Cook," he shouted. "Cook! Come here immediately."

The cook came scurrying and was very frightened when he heard the king's angry voice.

"You called, Your High mess…I mean, Your High nest….I mean Your Nigh pest…Oh dear! I don't know what I mean."

The king said, "Cook, from now on, the pancakes must be perfectly round, and all the peas on my plate must be in neat rows, and the peanut butter must be spread on my bread evenly, with no corners showing. Do you understand?"

"Y-y-y-yes, s-s-sir," the cook stammered. He ran from the king as fast as his legs would take him, through the kitchen, out the back door, and into the nearby forest, where he hid in the branches of the tallest tree he could find.

Meanwhile, the king had gone to his room to dress. When he opened his closet he saw hundreds of pairs of shoes, all different colors and styles.

"Shoemaker," he called out in a very loud voice.

The shoemaker came scurrying in and the king immediately scolded him.

"Shoemaker, you should not put shoes of different colors in the same closet. This is not neat at all. From now on, I want each color shoe to be in a different closet, neatly arranged. Do you understand?"

"But, Your Majesty, there aren't enough closets for all of the different colors and styles," the shoemaker said.

"Then build them," the king said, very impatiently.

"Yes, Your Highness; of course, Your Highness; certainly, Your Highness!!!" The frightened shoemaker ran out of the room as fast as he could, and didn't stop until he had reached the forest and climbed into the same tree as the cook, only one branch lower.

Next, the king walked into his gardens, but instead of being pleased with the beautiful plants and flowers, he was very upset. He called for the gardener.

"Gardener, this is a very messy garden. I want everything that grows here to be exactly the same size and shape. Anything that doesn't fit must be cut down immediately."

As soon as he could, the gardener ran out of the garden and into the forest where he climbed the tallest tree he could find, just one branch below the shoemaker.

The king went back into the castle to find the queen. He said, "My dear, you have always told me how important it is to be neat and tidy. Now that I am, I have decided to make a proclamation that anyone who isn't neat and tidy will have his head cut off."

"Oh my," the queen said. "What have I done? The king will have all of our heads cut off, and it will be my fault." She began to cry in great globs and sobs.

"Perhaps I can help," said a voice at her side. It was Joshua Thumbkins. "I know why you are crying, but I don't know what should be done. However, I know whom to ask. My youngest son is very wise. Very wise indeed."

He sped from the castle and returned with a young child.

"Your Highness," Thumbkins said, "I wish to introduce my son. He is only six years old, but when he was born a good fairy said to us, 'This child will be very, very wise, mark my words.' And so, that is what we named him. Marc-My-Words."

"Well, Marc," said the queen between tears, "if you are truly wise, please tell me what to do so that the king does not have all of our heads cut off."

The child thought for a moment and then he said, "I have a plan that I think may work." He whispered his plan to his father and the queen.

"Yes," they shouted with delight. "It's a very good plan." And the queen added, "Marc, you are a very wise child."

Joshua Thumbkins blushed at the compliment paid to his son, and bowed so low that his nose became caught in his shoelace and he could not straighten up. "Oh dear," said the queen, and she laughed out loud, the first good laugh she'd had in quite a while.

The next morning, when the king opened his closet it was filled with slippers all of one color, and all for the right foot, lined up in a neat row. He became very upset. "Where is my shoemaker?" he asked in a loud voice. "I can't walk around with slippers for only my right foot."

A servant came running. "Pardon, Your Highness, but the shoemaker ran away yesterday and he hasn't been seen since. But the queen told us that you wished all the slippers in your closet to be exactly the same, so we put the slippers for the left foot in a closet in the dungeon of the castle, until we could have a new closet made."

"Hmm," said the king. "Of course. That's the neatest thing to do." And he went into the depths of the castle, down to the cold and damp dungeon, where he found the match to his slipper. When he returned, he called for his cook.

"Cook, where are you? I'm hungry for my breakfast."

A servant came running. "Pardon, Your Highness, but we have not seen the cook since he ran into the forest yesterday, but the queen told us how to prepare your food." He brought the king a plate with one slice of bread.

The king became very annoyed. "Where is the rest of my breakfast? My pancakes and Swiss cheese?"

"Your Majesty, the queen said that the pancakes were not to be served because they were not perfectly round, and the cheese was not to be served because the holes were not all exactly the same size."

"Hmm," said the king. "Of course, she is right. But I think I'll stroll in my garden to clear my head. I don't feel very well."

When he got into the garden, all of the trees and the bushes and the flowers had been cut down, and there was no place he could sit in the shade. "Where is my gardener? Who has destroyed my garden?"

The queen appeared at his side. "Don't you remember, Your Majesty? You decreed that the trees and bushes would have to be cut down if they were not all exactly the same size. When the gardener heard that, he ran away and hasn't been seen since."

The king said, "Did I decree that? Now I have no gardener, no cook, no shoemaker. How could I be so foolish? This is terrible."

The queen said, "It is terrible, Your Majesty. And worse yet, you have issued a decree that anyone in the kingdom who is not neat and tidy will have his head cut off. The people are so frightened they are all planning to run and hide in the forest."

The king said. "I have not been a wise king." His face brightened. "But I know how to fix everything. I will issue another decree. From now on, anyone who is neat and tidy will have his head cut off."

The queen said, "That won't do at all."

The king became very sad. "Whatever I think of is terrible."

"Oh, no, Your Majesty," said Joshua Thumbkins, who appeared at his side. "You are a good king, and the people love you. But you have too many kingly things on your mind. You need an adviser to help you."

"Where will I find such an adviser?"

Thumbkins answered, "My youngest son is very wise."

"Yes," added the queen. "He would be a very wise adviser, mark my words."

At that moment, young Marc appeared and he bowed before the king. "Your Majesty," he said, "If you allow me to, I will serve you to the best of my ability."

The king said. "You're very young to be an adviser. I'll give you a test. What proclamation should I issue about neatness and tidiness in the kingdom?"

Marc answered, "You should issue a decree that says that each person in the kingdom should be just as neat and tidy as he or she chooses to be, and that there will be no cutting off of heads."

"Bravo," said the king. "Those are splendid suggestions. You are truly wise. From this moment on you will be the king's adviser."

All of the men and women in the kingdom cheered when they heard the good news. They shouted so loud that the cook, the shoemaker, and the gardener heard the cheers from where they were hiding and they tumbled out of the tree.

The king turned to Joshua Thumbkins and said, "You must be very proud to have such a wise son."

Joshua blushed. When he tried to thank the king, his tongue got caught in his tonsils and he had to eat gobs of ice cream and licorice before his tongue was freed.

The cook, the shoemaker, and the gardener laughed when they discovered they had all been in the same tree, and then they rushed back into the castle to serve the king once more.

But most of all, the king and the queen rejoiced that all was well, the kingdom had been saved, and they would live happily ever after. Mark my words.

# Dror and Parrot's Bar Mitzvah

DROR COOPER SHOCKED his parents: he announced that he wouldn't have his Bar Mitzvah. He had studied and practiced the prayers and Torah and Haftarah portion, and had prepared a speech and attended services religiously the last several months, but when the Shabbat approached for his own Bar Mitzvah, he declared he would not participate. He had too many doubts about religion, even about God. It would be hypocritical, he asserted, to lead the services or read from the Torah.

His parents pleaded with him. The invitations had gone out, guests were coming from far and wide, there was an elegant lunch planned after the services and a party in the evening. *Kippot* (head coverings) had been ordered, special *kippot* in maroon and black, Dror's own choice, with his name and the date inscribed in Hebrew on the inside. Besides, he was a Jewish child. He had to have his Bar Mitzvah. The family would be shamed if he didn't. Mr. Cooper threatened to ground Dror forever if he continued in his stubborn refusal. The pleading and threats had no effect. Dror insisted that on the day of his Bar Mitzvah he would go to the synagogue and sit next to his parents, but he would not lead the service. Nothing could persuade him.

On Shabbat the synagogue was filled with invited guests, friends, and family from all over, and the regulars who came every week. Dror came to synagogue too, dressed in the holiday clothes that his mother had painstakingly chosen for him, and sat in the front row reserved for the family. As the time approached to begin the services, the rabbi and the cantor looked at Dror, but he didn't budge from his seat.

The services had to begin. When they did, Dror heard a voice very much like his own intoning the prayers from the pulpit where he should have been, even though he was sitting silently in his seat. How could this be? He looked at his father, but his father refused to return his gaze. Surely there couldn't be a tape recorder in the synagogue, not on the Sabbath. People in the congregation stared at Dror, and then at the *bima* where the voice was coming from, and they were fascinated and puzzled. It was a mystery.

It was not a mystery to Dror's father. Before the Bar Mitzvah, his parents had asked Dror what gift he wanted for his special birthday. Dror had always wished to have a pet dog or cat, but he couldn't, because his younger brother was allergic. He finally told his parents he wanted a bird. Not just any kind of a bird, but a parrot. He had read about parrots and how they could learn to speak. There was even a story about a parrot who had once startled a burglar and caused him to flee a house in fright. At first his parents had objected, but finally they bought him a parrot from a pet shop owned by an Israeli. The shopkeeper told them that the bird, Tooki, was very clever, and had spent the first years of its life in the shopkeeper's own home until his daughter had gone off to college.

Dror tried to teach Tooki a few simple phrases: "Hello," "Hi Dror," "What's up?" but Tooki seemed incapable of learning. Other than an occasional squawk, the bird didn't offer a single recognizable utterance. Dror had urged his father to return Tooki to the pet shop, but with all of the excitement and preparations for the Bar Mitzvah, nothing had been done. The bird was apparently incapable of speech. It was mute, or so it seemed.

One afternoon while Dror was at school, Mr. Cooper played the tape the cantor had given Dror to prepare for his Bar Mitzvah. On the tape the cantor said the blessings and then had a blank period for Dror to repeat them. As he played the tape, Dror's father heard a voice from the next room imitating the cantor. It was Tooki. Amazingly, the parrot seemed to know the blessings perfectly. Dror's father now understood why Tooki hadn't spoken. Dror had been trying to teach Tooki English, but the parrot had spent most of its life hearing

Hebrew. While Dror had been practicing aloud in his room for his Bar Mitzvah, the parrot had learned the service by heart.

That was the seed of a wild plan that was hatched, with the rabbi's consent, when it seemed that Dror could not be persuaded to participate in his own Bar Mitzvah. Friday afternoon, Dror's father sneaked the parrot out of Dror's room and hid it behind the pulpit in the synagogue. When the parrot heard the congregation chanting in Hebrew it began reciting the words that Dror had practiced so often in his room. At first Dror couldn't believe his ears. He looked at his father again, and this time Mr. Cooper smiled. It was true. It really was his parrot leading the congregation in his place.

This was too much for Dror. He forgot his nervousness and his reservations. His Bar Mitzvah would not be conducted by a parrot! Dror jumped up from where he was sitting, threw a *tallit* (prayer shawl) over the parrot in its cage, and led the rest of the services himself. Afterwards, his parents and grandparents and all of the visitors remarked at how proud they were of him, how well he had done, and how unique this had been. It was certainly the first time in the history of that particular synagogue, and possibly any synagogue, that a parrot had shared the pulpit with a Bar Mitzvah and, at all the appropriate places, even though its voice was muffled, had said, "Amen."

# The Day the Ark Almost Sank

ONE DAY GOD LOOKED at the world and saw that except for Noah, the people were all mean and cruel to each other and even to their animals. He told Noah to build a huge ark for himself, his family, and each of the animal and bird species in the world. He was going to create a great flood and start the world all over again. For forty days and nights it rained and for a whole year the whole earth was covered with water. Only the people and the animals in the ark were saved. If God hadn't told Noah to build that ark, how lonely and empty this world would be. Everything and everybody would have drowned. There would be no dogs or cats, no llamas, no mice, no kangaroos, and worst of all, no *you*.

Life on the ark wasn't easy. For more than a year all of the creatures of the world had to live together, and many of them hardly knew each other. None of the animals had been friends with a snake before, and the baboon had never even seen a polar bear. Some of the animals were used to staying up all night. They had to learn to sleep when it was dark so they wouldn't disturb the others. There were some things Noah hadn't thought of when he was building the ark. For example, the giraffe wanted the mirror high so that he could admire himself while brushing his teeth in the morning, but the little animals, like the chipmunks and the squirrels, could only see themselves by scurrying up the wall until Noah provided little mirrors for them.

At dinnertime they all sat around one long table and by the time the food got to the hippo and the walrus, it was two days old and not very tasty. There were lots of complaints that the food was too cold or too hot or too mushy or too hard to chew.

At night, each animal had its own bunk, some on the top and some on the bottom so there would be room for everyone. Noah put a little card on each of the bunk beds so the animals would know where they belonged. But the monkeys had to make mischief. They took the name cards off the bunks one night and mixed them up. When the animals went to their bunks, they became all confused and kept bumping into each other in the dark. At last each found his name tag and, very tired, lay down to sleep. But those mischievous monkeys changed the cards so that the little animals were in the bottom bunks and the huge animals were in the top ones. The rhino was sleeping above the kitten and almost made a flat cat of the poor thing. The elephant's trunk hung down over the mouse and tickled the creature all night. The giraffe had no room at all for his long neck and was stiff and sore the next day.

But the worst and scariest was when the ark almost sank and everyone in it nearly drowned. On that day there was a fierce storm. The sky grew dark and the winds tossed the ark from side to side. Even the elephant could hardly stand. The waves carried the ark high into the sky, and then it came crashing down. The hippos bellowed and the mice squeaked and even the mighty lions were afraid.

Noah herded all the animals out of the wind and rain and into the bottom of the ark. "Move quickly," he said, "but be calm. No pushing or shoving. Help each other."

The sharp-eyed leopard let out a loud roar. "What's the matter?" Noah asked. The leopard was too frightened to speak. Instead, he roared again, and pointed to a hole in the side of the ark. Water was trickling in, and getting deeper and deeper. Something had to be done immediately or the ark would sink!

*First the seal dove down in the pool of water.*
*She found a hole, the size of a quarter.*
*The beavers cut plugs from the dining room table.*
*The horses brought hay they had saved from their stable.*
*The monkeys ran around, gathering twigs.*

*The shy bald eagles donated their wigs.*

Noah took the hay, the plugs, the wigs, the twigs, pressed them into the hole, and sealed it with oatmeal that was left over from breakfast. Everyone took a hand or a paw or a wing or a flipper and patted the patch into place. Outside, the wind was still blowing fiercely and the ark was rocking and shaking and groaning, and sounded like it might break into a million pieces. Noah said a prayer.

*What a lonely place,*
*This world will be,*
*If this ark and the animals,*
*Go down in the sea.*
*So, God, if You love us,*
*And we know You do,*
*Please don't let that water get through!*

When Noah finished his prayer, the sea grew calm and the ark seemed to breathe a sigh of relief. Everyone in it breathed a sigh of relief. The elephant lifted its trunk and made a loud blast of thanks that sounded like the *shofar* at the end of the fast on Yom Kippur. Everyone climbed out into the open air and saw a most wonderful sight. Instead of dark clouds and pouring rain, they saw a rainbow from one end of the sky to the next. They knew they were saved. The flood was over.

It took awhile before they could get off the ark because the water was still too deep. When the land was dry and it was safe to leave, the animals hugged each other and said goodbyes as they went back to their favorite places, the trees, the jungle, the desert, the farm, or back into the sea. And there they remain. But every now and then, after a great storm, when a rainbow covers the whole sky, they remember the time long ago when they all lived together, and how all did their part on the day the ark almost sank.

# Now You Are Three

ONCE THERE WAS A little boy named Jacob who was two years old. When people asked, "How old are you?" he showed them two fingers. But he didn't say a word.

His mommy said, "Tell them how old you are, Jacob."

Jacob put up two fingers, but he didn't say a word.

His daddy said, "Jacob, tell them how old you are. Are you two years old?"

Jacob nodded his head and held out two fingers. He looked down at his two fingers, but he didn't say a word.

Jacob knew his colors, how to count, and how to sing "Shabbat Shalom," but he just didn't feel like telling people how old he was. So, when they asked, he never said a word.

One day in June, Jacob and his mommy and daddy and Baby Elana went for a walk. A lady came up to him and said, "My, what a nice boy you are. I'll bet you are two years old."

Jacob looked at the woman. She was wearing a pretty green hat, and she was smiling at him. Jacob didn't hold up two fingers. And he didn't nod his head. Because something had changed.

He said to the lady, "I used to be two years old but I just had a birthday and now I'm three."

His mommy and daddy said, "That's right, Jacob, now you are three."

Baby Elana said, "Wa, wa, wa." Maybe she knew that Jacob was three years old, too. Or maybe she just wanted her bottle.

Now when people say to Jacob, "How old are you?" he holds up three fingers and he says, "I am three."

# The Four Questions

JACOB ALWAYS ASKED QUESTIONS. "Why does the sun come out during the day, and the moon at night?" "Why don't apples grow in the ground, like potatoes?" "Why does Elana have straight hair, and mine is curly?" "Why are some kids so mean?" "Why can't I put my underwear on my head?" "Why can't I wear my coat inside out?" Why, why, why.

His tired daddy said, "Jacob, you keep interrupting me. I'm trying to relax and read the newspaper. I don't want to answer any more questions. As a matter of fact, I'd appreciate it if you didn't ask any more for a whole month."

On Passover, Jacob went to visit his grandma and grandpa. Lots of people were sitting at the table for the Passover seder. The tablecloth was white and had nice dishes and glasses and silverware. There was wine on the table, too.

Grandpa lifted his cup of wine. All the other people lifted their cup of wine. Grandpa said the blessing over the wine. Then Grandpa said, "Who is going to ask the Four Questions?"

Jacob's mommy said, "Jacob knows the Four Questions."

Grandpa looked at Jacob and said, "Are you going to ask the Four Questions?"

Jacob said, "No."

"Why not?" Grandpa asked. "Don't you know them?"

"I can't," Jacob said.

"Why not?" everybody asked.

"Because Daddy said I can't ask another question for a whole month."

Everyone looked at Daddy, but Daddy didn't look at anyone. He felt foolish. He said, "Jacob, I changed my mind. You can ask all the questions you want to."

Grandpa turned again to Jacob and said, "Now will you ask the Four Questions?"

Jacob did ask the Four Questions, in Hebrew and in English. Grandpa was very, very pleased. After that, Jacob asked many more questions, and nobody said he shouldn't.

# Jacob's Flying Birthday Party

TODAY IS JACOB'S BIRTHDAY and later in the afternoon there is to be a birthday party for him at his grandparents' home. His mom and dad were working in the garden, pulling weeds and planting vegetables. Jacob and Elana were playing in the backyard. It was warm, but there were dark clouds in the sky. It looked like rain again. It had rained yesterday and the day before. That's why Mom and Dad were so anxious to get the gardening done. It started to get darker and darker, and raindrops began to fall. Dad looked up at the sky.

"We'd better go inside," he said.

"Not yet. It's not raining hard," Elana said.

"Come," Mom said. "It's getting dark. It's going to pour in just a minute."

They all went inside after putting the toys and the tools away. Jacob noticed he had left his Berenstein Bears book on the picnic table. He didn't want it to get ruined in the rain. He ran out to get it.

While he was running, he had a strange sensation. His feet barely seemed to be touching the ground. The wind was blowing so hard it just carried him along. He tried to grab the book, but when he reached for it, he couldn't stop. The wind pushed him past it. His feet got further and further from the ground and he began to float up into the sky.

He looked down. His house was getting smaller. Someone was running out of the door waving at him. It was his dad.

He supposed his dad was shouting, "Come back! Come down!" but Jacob couldn't hear him.

Some children might have been frightened to be floating on the wind so high, but not Jacob. Just two days ago he had watched a bird in the sky and he had wished very hard that he could fly, if only for one day, to see what it was like, and so he wasn't even surprised to be flying. He thought it was just his wish coming true.

He wasn't at all sure how high he would go, or how he would get back home, but he figured that he could worry about all of those details later. For now, he concentrated on flying as well as possible. He discovered that if he dipped his body one way or the other, he could swoop and change directions. Even though it was raining, he was dry. He was flying above the rain.

"This is neat," he thought as he flew past his schoolyard and looked to see who was on the playground. It was full of puddles and no one was there. He kept on going and even circled back over his own house, but he couldn't see anyone. They were all out frantically searching for him.

The rain stopped and the wind began to die down, but instead of falling, Jacob found that he could fly without the wind. All he needed to do was to relax and to think high and mighty thoughts. That was easy for Jacob.

He tried to turn, but he dipped too sharply and soon he was going around and around in a great circle until he got dizzy and couldn't tell which way was up and which way was down. A robin flew by and looked at him curiously, wondering what kind of a strange bird Jacob was, and why he was flying upside down. The robin tried flying upside down too, but didn't like it.

Jacob got himself straightened around. Pretty soon he saw a sign that said, "Welcome to Iowa."

"Uh oh," Jacob thought, "I've gone much too far." He considered visiting Iowa to see what it was like, but he decided to do that another day. He'd have to get home pretty soon or his mom and dad would really start to worry about him. He turned north and headed for his grandma and grandpa's house.

Along the way he got into the middle of a gaggle of geese flying to Lake Harriet. The geese started to giggle when they saw Jacob. What a silly looking goose that one is, they thought. Jacob followed the giggling gaggle of geese all the way to Lake Harriet. They splashed down into the lake, but Jake kept circling until he spied the big water tower near his grandparents' home. He flew over the water tower and got a good look at the huge soldiers and fierce-looking birds carved on its surface. Then he turned towards his grandparents' home and saw his grandpa carrying a very large box into the house. The top of the box was open and Jacob could see that it was his birthday cake. He was seven years old today. Now he spotted his Grandma carrying a bunch of packages, all wrapped with fancy ribbons.

"I'll bet those are presents for me," he thought. "For my birthday."

If he landed in his grandma and grandpa's backyard, he would be just in time for his birthday party. He had one problem. He didn't know how to land. He thought, "What if I crash hard, and break all of my bones?" Suddenly, he no longer had high and mighty thoughts, and he started falling towards the ground. Down, down, down he came. Try as he might, he couldn't stop.

"Looooooook ooooout!!!!" He shouted as he plunged to the ground.

Grandma and Grandpa looked up in amazement. Grandpa quickly raced into the house and came back out carrying the ten-layer cake he had bought for Jacob's party.

Jacob kept falling. He was out of control. Grandpa raced under him, holding the cake. Jacob fell into the first layer of the cake, then the second and the third, and all way to the tenth layer. Then he stopped. His face was buried in cake and frosting and his feet were in the air, but he was safe. Jacob wriggled out of the cake. There was icing all over his face, sticking out of his ears, his nose, his mouth. Just then the geese flew over. They circled twice, happily honking "Happy birthday to you," before they took off into the sky.

Grandma and Grandpa were amazed at all that had happened. But the important thing was that Jacob was safe and had arrived just in time for his birthday party in their backyard. Pretty soon Dad and Mom and Elana came racing into the backyard, and they could also see that he was safe.

Of course they still had to figure out what they would use for a birthday cake, and where they would put the candles. Once they scraped Jacob clean, there was quite enough cake left to be shaped into a flying goose, and when the other children arrived soon after, they never knew the difference.

# Birthday Radio Broadcast

RADIO ANNOUNCER: Good morning, ladies and gentlemen. Here are the big news stories for today.

A boy in Eagan, Minnesota, brushed so vigorously that one of his teeth fell out, and went down the drain. An alligator swimming in the sewer swallowed the tooth and took off for Africa. The alligator spit out the tooth because it didn't like that brand of toothpaste. A man in Africa found the tooth and put it under his son's pillow that night, and the tooth fairy left him fifty cents. That was enough to buy rice for a whole week, and the family was saved from starvation. So, be sure to brush your teeth every morning, boys and girls.

A little girl in Eagan, Minnesota, was jumping rope. She jumped so high her hair caught on the branch of a tree. A bald eagle snatched some of the hair to make a wig. The other bald eagles didn't recognize him, so they kicked him out of the Eagle Scouts. The sad eagle folded his wings and refused to eat. He got so skinny that his head shrunk and the wig slipped off. The other eagles said, "Where have you been? We've been looking all over for you?" Then he flew away with the rest of the eagles and caught some yummy mice.

**We interrupt this broadcast to bring you a really important announcement.** Jacob Siegel is ten years old today. The president has declared a national holiday because of Jacob's birthday and has ordered that the U.S. Treasury issue a new three-dollar bill with Jacob's face on it. Wait! A bald eagle swooped down, stole all of the bills, and was then swallowed by an African alligator that was in the neighborhood. All of the new bills are gone. Instead, the president has proclaimed that anyone who comes in contact with Jacob Siegel this day is ordered to wish him a VERY HAPPY BIRTHDAY!

# It's a Math, Math World

Q. What was the Brilliant Math Student's favorite zoo animal?
A. The hippopotenuse.

Q. Who was the first mathematician?
A. God, because He said, "Be fruitful and multiply."

Q. What did the Brilliant Math Student say when the bird built a nest in his hair?
A. Ge-om-etry.

Q. Why did the Brilliant Math Student buy a cemetery plot?
A. Because his days were numbered.

Q. What kind of a table hasn't got a leg to stand on?
A. A multiplication table.

Q. What did the Brilliant Math Student do when she became a feminist?
A. Burned her Alge-bra.

Q. Why did the Brilliant Math Student throw away his eyeglasses?
A. Because they blurred di-vision.

Q. What kind of books did the Brilliant Math Student collect?
A. First additions.

Q. Why did the Brilliant Math Student go to the psychiatrist?
A. For a number of reasons.

# THE CHILDREN'S CORNER

Q. Why didn't the Brilliant Math Student join the discussion?
A. Because he had nothing to add.

Q. Why are Brilliant Math Students good at felling trees?
A. Because they've got loga-rhythm.

Q. Why was the foreign acrobat thrown out of the bank?
A. Because he couldn't balance his Czech book.

Q. Why didn't the Brilliant Math Student ever get where he wanted to go?
A. Because he always took a square route.

Q. Why didn't the Brilliant Math Student recognize an apple pie when he saw it?
A. Because he thought that all $\Pi r2$.

Q. Why did the Brilliant Math Student have to take a pill?
A. Because he had an arithme-tic.

Q. Why did your grandfather make up all these silly jokes?
A. Because he couldn't think of any really funny ones.
(And also because he loves and admires you very much!)

# The Lost Chord

CONSIDERING HOW IMPORTANT this day would be, Jacob was remarkably calm. He was scheduled to give a concert that evening at Carnegie Hall, representing his high school in a statewide competition. If all went well, he would quit high school and remain in Manhattan to pursue a career in music. No one knew of these plans except his sister, Elana, and she was sworn to secrecy. To be on the safe side, he had also locked her in a closet with duct tape over her mouth.

He was about to leave for the concert hall, but he had a nagging feeling he had forgotten something. He opened his briefcase once more and checked its contents: clean shirt, sheet music, shoehorn, directions to the hall. It was all there, but he still had a feeling of disquiet. Something was not right.

He looked in the briefcase once more and glanced through the music he planned to play. He immediately recognized the problem. On the final piece, "ShoeBert's Soleful Symphony," the final chord was missing. It had been there earlier, when he had been practicing, but in the hurry to pack and leave, he had misplaced it. This would never do. He couldn't end the concert without that chord.

He searched for it frantically. It wasn't on the piano bench, or on the piano itself. He lifted the top to see if it had gotten stuck in the sounding board. He pounded the keyboard to see whether the chord was trapped in the black keys, but all he heard were discordant notes. He was beginning to panic. He searched under his bed, in the dictionary under every combination of chord/cord he could find, in the base of the cordless telephone, in the closet where Elana was stuffed. She muttered something through the tape, but he ignored her. He had no time for conversation.

Jacob had to leave if he was to arrive at the concert hall on time. Reluctantly, he closed his briefcase and rushed to the subway, compulsively searching his pockets for the missing chord. He would have to rely on chance. Perhaps the chord would turn up while he was playing. If not, he didn't know what he would do as he came to the end of the piece. He couldn't omit the selection; it had been announced in the program and, besides, it was his most dazzling piece. He had to play it.

The concert began on time. Jacob was the first contestant and as he looked out at the audience, he could see music critics from the major newspapers and magazines. He began with "Sounds of Mew-Sick" from the Broadway musical *Cats*, and followed with "Overture to Car Men, with Horns and the Squealing of Brakes." The audience responded enthusiastically.

The applause from the previous songs died down and he could sense the excitement in the hall as they waited for his rendition of "ShoeBert's Unfinished Soleful Symphony for Piano and Shoehorn," the selection that had won him several awards, including a first in the coveted Richard Dyer-Bennet contest. He feared what would happen when he came to that climactic closing chord. He could see his hands suspended above the piano with no place to go, the audience becoming increasingly restless, irritated, and angry as he left them dangling.

He prayed for deliverance, and began. The notes flew into the air. He was inspired. His anxiety prompted him to push himself as he never had before. He played brilliantly, effortlessly blending piano and shoehorn. He came to the concluding passage and he could almost weep as he approached the final chord—an unfinished symphony with a lost chord! He held his hand in the air, waiting for a miracle, waiting for the chord suddenly to appear.

From the back of the room he could hear garbled sounds. It was his sister, Elana. She had escaped from the closet and somehow gotten herself to the auditorium. She ripped the duct tape from her mouth, and out came a resonant, melodic, thrilling chord, the final, missing chord. It had been trapped in her mouth ever since she had stood by the piano during Jacob's earlier practice session at home. She knew it was there and had tried to tell Jacob before he left, but he ignored her. She had left the tape on until this moment so that the chord wouldn't emerge at the wrong time. She knew just where in the performance it belonged. Jacob finished triumphantly and the audience went wild. He raced to the back of the room and brought his sister forward. Together, they acknowledged the applause. Jacob unanimously earned a first in the competition.

Though he had offers to teach at one of the major music conservatories, Jacob decided to return home and complete his last year of high school. He and his sister are collaborating on an ambitious project that combines their love for music and their concern for the environment. They are attempting to create a unique song-cycle—that is, a two-wheeled vehicle that is propelled by song. If they succeed, congestion and noise pollution in America's cities may be a thing of the past. The roads and streets will be filled with the glorious sounds of music as businessmen, students, housewives, young and old, make their way from place to place with a melody in their hearts and a song on their lips.

# To Be or Not to Be—
## Seven Years Old

ELANA WASN'T SURE SHE wanted to be seven years old. After all, she had enjoyed being six quite a bit, and she couldn't be certain that seven would be half as nice. This last year she had started taking piano lessons, continued her dancing, was in scouts, and athletics, and was one of the biggest girls in her class. And she had lost so many baby teeth the tooth fairy was exhausted for having to visit her house so often. What could seven possibly offer that was as good as being six?

Elana decided not to rush into this business of growing up. She would have to think it over first, and discuss it with some other people.

First she spoke to her brother Jacob. "I'm thinking about skipping my birthday this year, Jacob, and not turning seven. What do you think?"

Jacob didn't like that idea at all. "If you do that, you won't have a party, and you won't get any presents for me to play with."

Next she decided to ask her mother. "That's an interesting idea," her mother said. "If you don't turn seven you'll stay my little girl, and I like that. And also, I won't have to clean up the house for a birthday party for all your friends. I especially like that."

Her dad was very enthusiastic. "If you don't want to have your seventh birthday, can I have it instead of you? And blow out the candles? And make the wish? And have my favorite meal? And get all the presents? And decide on which games to play? And not have to help clean up after? And eat as much candy as I wish? And not go to work that day? And……."

Elana interrupted him. "Wait a minute, Daddy. Wait a minute. I just changed my mind. You'll have to wait for November, for your own birthday. I've decided I really do want to be seven, and I really do want to have my own birthday party."

So, she had her birthday after all, a great party, and everyone who came had a wonderful time, especially Elana Rose Siegel, who was seven years old.

# The Adventures of Elana Siegel

CHAPTER 1

ELANA HAS HAD MANY adventures during her lifetime. The first adventure was when she had to decide when to be born, and which family to be born into. She could have picked almost any date within the year, but she chose March because it is such a dreary month in Minnesota, and she wanted to bring joy to some family. In March everyone is looking forward to spring, and instead there is another twenty inches of snow and the cars are buried and the flowers can't be planted, and the streets look gray and dirty. Yes, March was a good month to brighten some family's life—but which family?

She had lots of choices. There was a monkey family in the zoo that wanted to have a child and she considered it seriously for awhile because she knew how much fun monkeys have jumping around and making faces at the people. But then she decided she wouldn't want to be stuck in the zoo all of the time and it would frankly be a lot of work keeping her tail well groomed and clean. A ponytail seemed like a better idea.

She heard about a family in Burnsville that had twelve boys and desperately wanted a girl. She decided not to join them. She could imagine she would be a better soccer player than the boys and that might make them unhappy.

The family Siegel in Eagan already had a boy named Jacob, and was very interested in adding a girl. Jacob seemed like a pretty cool character and she figured she would get along with him (most of the time). He didn't like tomatoes, and that was good because she could pick those out of any salads for herself. Wearing two different socks wouldn't be any problem at all because the dad in this family did it quite often without intending to. And the mom was great in arts and crafts and that would be fun as she grew older. Oh, and there were some grandparents, too, who looked like the types who would be willing to spoil her; that was in their favor, too.

She selected the Siegel family, and on March 1, 1991 she floated down, moved right in, chose the name Elana (and let the parents think they had chosen it), started shaping that family up, and they are coming along pretty well though her work certainly isn't finished yet.

## CHAPTER 2. SCHOOL DAYS

Deerwood School is a very pleasant-looking, modern school. Early in the morning and later in the afternoon the parking lot is filled with buses taking children to and from the neighborhood. Elana Siegel, the hero of our story, did not usually take the bus, but one day she was going to play at her friend Kim's house after school and so she boarded the bus with Kim.

"Did you notice that bus driver?" Kim asked. "He looked a little weird to me."

The two girls took seats in the back of the bus and didn't pay any more attention to the driver. They were too busy talking about the fun they were going to have for the rest of the afternoon.

After awhile, Kim noticed that they were not on the usual route, and the ride was taking much too long. Something was wrong. The girls looked more carefully at their bus driver and discovered it wasn't a person at all. Sitting in the driver's seat, wearing a bus driver's cap and uniform, was a large Canadian goose. And none of the passengers were children. They were all ducks and geese and assorted birds. Elana spoke to the driver.

"What's going on here? Where are we headed?" she asked.

The driver honked the horn, "We're going south. This is the bus that takes birds and waterfowl to the South for the winter—the ones who are too old or sick to fly by themselves."

"But that's not where we're going," Elana and Kim said together. "We've got to get home, back to Eagan."

"Sorry," the bus-goose said. "I'm not allowed to make any stops. It's against the rules. You'll just have to go to the South with the rest of us. We should be there in a couple of days."

"What are we going to eat?" Kim asked.

"No problem," the driver said. "We have enough seeds and worms for everyone."

At that moment, the girls knew they had to get off that bus and get back home, even though it would have been interesting to get a bird's-eye view of the South.

"I have an idea," Elana whispered to Kim.

"Go for it," said Kim.

Elana went up to the driver once more. "Excuse me, Mr. Goose-driver," she said, "but I'm afraid you will have to take us back to the school where you picked us up. It's in the rules."

"What rules?" asked the driver.

"The migratory bird rules," Elana said. "You see, I am a Siegel, and Siegels are not migratory birds, and so we are not allowed on this bus."

"Are you sure?" asked the driver.

"Absolutely," said Elana, even though she really wasn't.

"Well, OK, then," the driver said. "We birds are law-abiding citizens."

So, he turned the bus around and brought the children right up to Kim's house. Kim's mother was waiting as the children got off the bus.

"What took you so long?" she asked.

"Should we tell her?" Elana asked Kim.

"Nah. She'd never believe it," Kim answered.

"OK," Elana said. "Let's go play."

The children went into the house, had a nice snack that Kim's mother had prepared, and chuckled when they thought of eating worms and birdseed, but they didn't say anything about their adventure. This is the first time anyone has heard of it.

CHAPTER 3. (Maybe someday it will get written).

# Allison's Birthday Party

A TURTLE WAS WALKING along the side of the road. He was going to Allison's birthday party, but turtles move very slowly and even though it was not far, he had already been walking for a long time.

"Oh dear, I'll never get to Allison's house in time for the party," he said to himself. "I should have started yesterday."

Along the way Turtle spotted a large bird gathering berries that were growing near the road.

"Excuse me, Mrs. Bird, but I am late for Allison's birthday party. I wonder if you could fly me there."

The bird had a ripe, blue berry in its mouth and couldn't talk until it had tilted its head back and swallowed the berry.

"Umm. That was delicious. Would you like one?" asked the bird.

"Thank you. I would like it berry—I mean very much, but only one, please. I don't want to spoil my appetite. I think Allison will have birthday cake at her party."

"Climb on my back," said the bird, "and I'll fly you to the party."

Turtle was too heavy and the bird couldn't fly

Soon they passed a small dog running along a ditch on the side of the road.

"Where are you going?" he asked.

"To Allison's birthday party," they said, "but we're going to be very late."

Dog said, "If you let me come too, I'll carry you both on my back and run the whole way." But when Turtle tried to climb on Dog's back, Dog let out a yelp and said, "Oof, please get off. You're too heavy. Why are you so heavy?"

Turtle answered, "It's because of the piano. I brought along a piano to play 'Happy Birthday' to Allison."

"Do you know how to play the piano?" asked Bird. "If you can play 'Happy Birthday,' I can sing it very well."

"Not really," said Turtle, "But I'm sure someone else at the party will know how to play."

Dog walked along with Turtle, and Bird flew overhead. Turtle continued to fret that they would be too late for the party and that there would be no birthday cake left when they arrived.

They saw a man sitting at the side of the road. "Where are you going?" he asked.

Dog answered, "We are going with Turtle to Allison's birthday party, but we are going to be late because Turtle moves so slowly."

The man said, "I am a musician. If there is a piano at Allison's house, I could play 'Happy Birthday' when we get there, if I can come too."

"Turtle is carrying a piano along with her," said Bird. "And you can play it when we get to Allison's house if you want to come along with us."

Turtle and Bird and Dog and the musician all continued to Allison's house. They passed a small boy sitting next to his wagon at the side of the road. The boy looked sad.

"What's the matter?" the musician asked.

"My wagon is stuck. It won't go."

The musician said, "If I can get your wagon unstuck, will you let Turtle ride in it while we all go to Allison's party?"

"I would love to," said the boy, "but how will you get my wagon unstuck from the mud?"

"I'll show you," he said. The musician reached gently into the house that Turtle was carrying on his back and started playing a song on the piano:

MERRILY WE ROLL ALONG, ROLL ALONG, ROLL ALONG.
MERRILY WE ROLL ALONG,
TO ALLI'S BIRTHDAY PARTY!

As soon as he started playing, the wagon became unstuck and began merrily to roll along.

"Hooray!" everyone shouted.

The little boy jumped into the wagon with Turtle on his lap. Dog ran beside it, and the musician pulled as fast as he could. Bird flew overhead and showed them the way. They ran until they came to Allison's house. The little boy jumped out of the wagon and ran to the door.

Allison came out and said, "Hello, everybody. Come in. You're just in time for my party."

They all did, except Bird. As soon as she saw Marlee, Allison's cat, she decided it would be very comfortable to wait outside in the backyard. Turtle was very happy to see that the birthday cake hadn't been cut yet and the candles hadn't been lit.

Mommy lit the candles. Daddy took pictures with his video camera. The musician played "Happy Birthday" on Turtle's piano and they all sang. Bird sang very sweetly and very loudly because she was outside in the backyard, and wouldn't come in. Allison blew out the candles with a little help from Turtle. Everyone had as much cake as they wanted, even Turtle, and Allison threw crumbs outside so that Bird could have some too.

Bapa and Mae Mae weren't there, but they wished they were. They sent Allison this birthday story instead.

# Elijah's Cup

THE DINING ROOM TABLE was set with the special dishes and the fancy tablecloth that Grandma used only on Passover. When the seder began, each person at the table had a kiddush cup, even the children. There was a kiddush cup in the middle of the table, too. It was the prettiest of them all. Allison, almost five years old, noticed it just when her grandfather said, "Allison, are you ready to ask the Four Questions?"

Instead of answering, Allison asked her grandfather, "Bapa, who is that cup for?"

"That's Elijah's cup. We'll come to that later in the seder. Now it's time to ask the Four Questions."

"Who is Elijah? Is he coming to our seder?"

"Of course. Elijah comes to everybody's seder. But not until later. Now we have to hear the Four Questions."

Allison looked puzzled. "How can Elijah go to everyone's seder, all at the same time?"

"It's a miracle," Grandpa said. "And do you want to know another miracle?"

"Sure," Allison said.

"Well, another miracle is your grandmother's matzoh ball soup. But if we don't hear the Four Questions soon, we'll never get to that miracle."

Allison said, "Bapa, don't joke. I want to know about Elijah."

"Answer her, Dad," Allison's mother said. "We are supposed to ask questions at the seder."

Grandfather said, "But 'seder' means order, and that question is out of order."

Allison's father interjected, "We told the children to ask lots of questions at the seder, not just the Four Questions."

Grandfather said, "All right, Allison, I'll tell you about Elijah. He lived a long time ago. He was a great Jewish prophet."

"What's a prophet, Bapa?"

"A wise and good man who had a message from God. He told everyone that God wants us to help poor and sick people. Now his spirit visits every seder and even though we can't see him, he sips the wine that's left for him in a special cup, like the one in the middle of our table. It's called Elijah's cup."

"When will he come?" Allison asked.

"Later in the seder we'll open the door for Elijah and invite him in. You can be the one who opens the door."

"And that's when he sips the wine?" Allison wanted to know.

"Yes. That's when he takes a sip of wine. You look carefully at the cup, and you'll see that a little bit is gone after we invite Elijah in."

Allison thought for awhile. "Couldn't we invite him for the whole seder, Bapa? I could make room for him next to me."

"Oh, but he has so many seders to visit, Allison, it wouldn't be fair to keep him here all night."

Allison nodded. She was thinking about Elijah and his special cup.

Her grandfather said, "Any more questions, Allison?"

"Yes," Allison answered. Then she asked the Four Questions in Hebrew. Everyone was very proud of her.

Later, Allison opened the door for Elijah. When she returned to her place, she could see that a little of the wine in Elijah's cup was gone. Uncle Josh, who was sitting right there, was sure she was right. He smiled and said he saw the wine go down with his own two eyes.

Everyone laughed, including three-year-old Zachary, because he liked to laugh when the other people did. Allison thought she heard Elijah laughing too, but it was hard to tell with all the noise.

"Next year," she thought to herself, "I'm going to listen and watch very carefully."

# A Tree for Rosh Hashanah

WHEN IT WAS CLOSE to Rosh Hashanah, the Jewish New Year, Allison Jacobs, who was nine years old, came home from Hebrew school and told her mother and father she wanted to plant a tree in their backyard.

"Why?" her parents asked.

"Because of the Rosh Hashanah story my teacher told us today."

"What story?" her father asked.

"The story of the carob tree."

"I don't know that story," her mother said. "Tell it to us."

"I don't know if I remember it exactly," Allison said, "but it's about a little girl and an old man and a tree. The little girl was walking along and saw an old man digging in his garden. She stopped and watched for awhile, and then she said to the old man, 'What are you doing?' And the old man answered, 'Getting ready to plant a carob tree.' 'Why are you doing that?' the girl asked. 'Because it will give good shade' the man answered. The girl thought about that for awhile and then said, 'But you're old. You won't be here to sit in the shade of the tree.' That sounded kind of rude, but the old man didn't mind. 'That's true,' he said, 'but it will be there for my children and grandchildren. That's who I'm planting it for.'"

"That's a nice story," Allison's parents said, "but why is it a Rosh Hashanah story?"

"My teacher said it's because on Rosh Hashanah we should think about what we can do to bring comfort to other people, like the old man did."

"That's very nice, dear, but we are awfully busy today and don't have time to plant a tree."

"That's all right," Allison said, "I'll do it myself."

Allison hadn't ever seen a carob tree, but she figured that "carob" sounded very much like "carrot" so the first thing she did was to plant a carrot in her backyard where they had a garden last year. After awhile something did sprout from the ground, but it didn't look like a tree at all and anyway, a rabbit chewed off the top.

Then she thought that perhaps some other sort of tree would be just as good. "Mommy," she asked, "Where do oak trees come from?"

"From acorns," her mother said.

The next time Allison went grocery shopping with her Mom she asked her to buy some fresh corn. She planted one kernel of corn—"a-corn"—in the garden right next to where the carrot had been. She watered it faithfully and checked every day, but this time nothing grew at all and even the rabbit wasn't interested.

Later, when she was walking with her father, she saw a different kind of tree. "Daddy," she said. "What's the name of that tree?"

"I think it's an ash tree," he said.

Allison knew where to get ashes. She scooped some out of the fireplace and carefully planted them in the backyard, alongside the carrot and the "a-corn." She watered faithfully and checked every day, but the ashes turned into mud and no tree grew.

In the next several days, Allison planted some maple syrup hoping to get a maple tree, an aspirin hoping to get a "sick-no-more" tree, and some hair from her cat, hoping it would turn into a fur tree, but nothing grew except weeds and grass. She was very discouraged.

"What's the matter, Alli?" her mother asked.

"I wanted to plant a tree for future generations to enjoy," Allison said, "but nothing I planted grew."

"Planting a tree is very nice," her mother said, "but there are other things you can do for Rosh Hashanah."

"Like what?" Allison asked.

"Well, you can help me bake some cookies and bring them to Dick next door because he hasn't been feeling very well and it will cheer him up."

"Is that like planting a carob tree?" Allison asked.

"I think so," her mother said, "because it is an act of kindness and will make him happy. Ask Zachary to come with you when you deliver the cookies. Then your brother will remember what you did and will be kind to someone else, and so it gets passed on from one person and from one generation to the next, just like the carob tree."

Allison thought about that for awhile, and then she called out, very loudly, "Zachary, come here for a minute."

"What do you want?" Zachary called back.

"I want to tell you a story."

"What kind of story?" Zachary asked.

"It's about a little boy and a carob tree," Allison answered.

"A carrot tree?" Zachary asked.

"No, a carob tree. Come on over and I'll tell it to you."

"Cool," Zachary said.

Later that evening, when Zachary's dad was putting him to bed, his father said, "Do you want me to read you a story?"

Zachary answered, "No, Dad, tonight I want to tell you a story."

"What's it about?" his dad asked.

"It's about an old man and a little boy and a funny kind of tree."

"That sounds cool," his father said.

# Zachary Goes for a Ride

ZACHARY LOVES TRUCKS. One day he decided to build a truck out of blue and yellow blocks. At first it didn't look much like a truck, but then he mixed up some imagination and dabbed it on the blocks until they became a fine truck. He decided to take his truck for a ride in the neighborhood.

As soon as he started, he saw a bird on the ground in his backyard.

"What's the matter?" Zachary asked.

"I fell out of my nest and I can't get back."

Zachary said, "I can help. With a little more imagination I can give my truck a front shovel."

"Is that really a truck?" the little bird asked.

"Of course it is," Zachary said. "Now climb into the shovel."

The bird did and Zachary carefully lifted the shovel towards the branch of the tree and gently put the bird back in its nest.

"Thank you," the bird said.

Zachary rode his truck out of his backyard and into the street. He saw lots of race cars going in the same direction. He followed them to a race track.

"We are having a race," the driver of one of the cars said.

"Can I race too, in my truck?"

"Are those blue and yellow blocks really a truck?" the driver asked.

"Of course they are," Zachary answered.

"OK. Then you can race too."

Zachary's truck wasn't very fast. It came in last in the race. The race car driver came up to him and said, "Congratulations. You won the prize for LAST PLACE."

Zachary was very proud. He had never won a racing prize before.

He was on his way home when he saw a boy at the side of the road.

"What's the matter?" Zachary asked.

"I'm afraid to cross the road because there are too many cars."

"Don't worry," Zachary said. "Climb into the front shovel on my truck and I'll help you cross the road."

The boy stopped crying. "Is that really a truck? It looks like a bunch of yellow and blue blocks."

"Of course it is," Zachary said. "All you need is some imagination."

"I have lots of imagination," the boy said.

"Then climb into the shovel and I'll lift you to the other side."

The boy climbed in and Zachary carefully lifted the shovel across the road and put the boy safely on the other side.

"Thank you," the boy said, and he ran home.

Zachary decided to go home too. He rode his truck along the street until he came to his own backyard. He saw the bird again, but this time it was not on the ground. The bird was very excited.

"I'm flying. I'm flying."

Zachary said, "That's wonderful."

Zachary drove his truck back into his basement. His daddy came home from work and saw the yellow and blue blocks. "What a nice truck. Did you make that truck yourself?"

"Yes, I did."

"I'll bet that truck could take you to some interesting places."

"It already helped me rescue a bird and a little boy and it even won me a prize in a race." His father was very proud of him and he gave Zachary a great big hug.

The next day Zach decided to build a space rocket. This time he used the brown and red blocks, and lots more IMAGINATION.

# Assorted Poems With Children In Mind

# Colic*

The colic is a mystery;
The doctors don't know why,
When Baby should be sleeping,
Instead he starts to cry.

The way to cure the colic,
Presents a big dilemma,
But Dr. Spock opined that,
It helps to give an enema.

I read the enema instructions;
I put Baby in the right position,
He kicked, he screamed, he hollered,
Which ruined my disposition.

I wrote my mom a letter,
I said, Baby's acting frisky,
She said he might do better
With just a drop of whisky.

I took my mom's advice,
The whisky worked real fine,
So now I fill my glass,
When Baby starts in cryin'.

Temperance is a virtue,
And whisky is a sin,
But liquor will not hurt you,
If it's only medicine.

If Baby's got the colic,
And cries to raise the roof,
To stabilize your systolic,
Just increase the proof.

Well, Baby lost the colic,
But I'm still on the cure,
For though he's long since married,
Some habits will endure.

*If you have the strength, can be sung to the tune of "Logger Lover."

ASSORTED POEMS

# Rain

It rained today,
Yesterday too.
If it rains tomorrow,
What should I do?

I could carry an umbrella,
That might be good.
I could carry an umbrella,
Do you think I should?

# Koala

Koala, Koala,
Up in that tree,
I'll give you a dollar,
If you'll play with me.

But how will I get there?
It's too high to climb.
I'll stand on a tall chair
And reach for a rhyme.

ASSORTED POEMS

# Giraffe

I climbed up high,
In a very big tree,
To greet a giraffe
I wanted to see.

When I reached the eye,
Of that tall giraffe,
I looked him over,
But I only saw half.

I said "Howdy do!"
Then I slithered on down,
Until both my feet
Were back on the ground.

When I looked up now
—This will make you smile—
I found that I'd traveled
More than a mile.

# The Shrinking Giraffe

Do you remember that giraffe,
The one who made you laugh?
Well, he's not the same at all.
He's no longer very tall.

He's no longer very high,
And the doctors don't know why.
But I really think I do.
It's all because of you.

He wants to come and play,
He'll be coming any day;
And it really isn't fair
If his head's up in the air.

So he shrunk to be your height,
To a size that is just right.
And the two of you will play
For as long as he can stay.

And when the day is through,
And he goes back to the zoo,
He'll stretch his neck and then
He'll be very tall again.

The next time he comes by,
He will look and say, "Oh my!
I don't have to shrink at all,
Because Allie's grown so tall."

# Cats

We once had a cat,
A long time ago,
Why we got that cat
I really don't know.

It didn't chase mice,
It wasn't much good.
It didn't even purr
Like a real cat should.

In the middle of the night,
It climbed on my face.
It gave me a fright,
What a great disgrace!

Now, what was its name?
I just can't recall,
But I'm glad he's gone,
I don't miss that cat at all.

# Last Night I Saw the Moon

Last night I saw the moon
When I looked up in the sky.
I said, "Hello, Mr. Moon,
I'm glad that you came by."

Much to my surprise,
—It never happened before—
The moon spoke to me,
As I opened up the door.

He said, "Bapa, did you know,
Your Alli has been sick?"
I answered him, "Oh no.
"That's an awful, nasty trick."

I said, "Tell me, Mr. Moon,
What could the sickness be?"
He said, "She'll be better soon,
Just you wait and see."

I left the moon outside,
We didn't talk any more.
"Don't leave me here," he cried.
But he couldn't fit through my door.

So I left him in the sky.
That's where the moon belongs.
But the next time he comes by,
I'll sing him a cheery song.

# Now You Are Two

When you were none,
There was much to be done,
And little time for fun.

When you were one,
There was more to be done,
And always on the run.

Now that you're two,
Everything's new,
Because of you, Jacob.
Because of you!

# Zachary at Five

There once was a fellow named Zach
Who sat, by mistake, on a tack.
He jumped up so high,
He got lost in the sky
And it took him a week to get back.

ASSORTED POEMS

# Elana Is Six

What can I do?
I've tried and I've tried.
But my silly old shoe
Keeps coming untied.

Maybe some glue,
Smeared over the lace,
A big glob of glue
May keep it in place.

Oh dear! Bad luck!
Glue every place,
And the tongue of the shoe
Is stuck to my face

When I whistle or talk,
My shoe flops around,
And I can hardly walk
With my tongue near the ground.

Oh what a fix,
I've got to get free,
It's making me sick,
What my shoe did to me.

What to do now?
I've got an idea.
I think I know how
I can get myself clear.

Won't you come close?
I can show you neat tricks.
Hah! The shoe's on YOUR nose,
Elana who is turning six.

# I Planted Some Flowers

I planted some flowers
In my garden today,
Then I turned on the hose
And I watered all day.

My shoes were muddy,
And my hands got dirty,
But the plants took root
And were very sturdy.

The sun came out,
And the flowers bloomed.
I picked some nice ones
And put them in my room.

My neighbor said,
"Aren't those pretty?
If I can't have some
It will be a pity."

So I went in my garden
And gave her a few.
There weren't many left
By the time I was through.

The flowers were gone,
Except for one,
That had drunk lots of rain
And been blessed by the sun.

It smelled so fine,
And the color was gold,
Zach's favorite color,
Or so I've been told.

It reminds me of Zach,
So lovely and fine,
I'm sure glad he's
A grandson of mine.

# Tradition

In our tradition,
We have heroines galore,
And now is a good time,
To celebrate one more.

Eve was the first,
As everyone knows,
She lived in the Garden
And didn't shop for clothes.

If she had seen that apple,
But decided not to take it,
I guess that we would still
Be running around naked.

Mother Sarah laughed,
And she was full of mirth
When the angel told her
She was going to give birth.

She said, "But I'm ninety,
That can never be."
And God said, "Don't you worry,
Leave the miracles to Me."

Abraham sent his servant
To get Isaac a bride,
So he climbed on his camel
And took a long ride.

When he got to Canaan
He immediately could tell
That Rebecca was the one,
When he saw her at the well.

Miriam interceded
With Pharaoh's lovely daughter
When the Egyptian princess
Drew Moses from the water.

And later when the Israelites,
Crossed the Red Sea
She taught them a dance
To a new melody.

Moses had a wife
Whose name was Zipporah.
We don't know much about her
But I really think we oughta.

 Ruth was very loyal
To her mother-in-law,
She gave up her own people.
Who could ask for more?

"I will go where you go,"
She said to Naomi,
"Your people will be mine,
"You only have to show me."

Mordechai told Queen Esther
The terrifying news
That Haman was plotting
To exterminate the Jews.

So she bravely sought the king
To convince Ahashuerus
To hang Haman instead
And make a decree to spare us.

All these special women
Did very important things,
But none surpass Elana
For the pleasure that she brings.

# Purim Poem

Ahashuerus was a foolish king,
Wine and carousing was his thing.
He invited Queen Vashti to come to a ball,
But he told her to dress in nothing at all.
She boldly refused, and so instead,
He commanded his men to cut off her head.
A headless queen was not much fun,
So he searched around for another one.

Of all the beauties in Shushan Land,
Esther was the one he offered his hand.
 "Remember you're a Jew," said Mordecai,
"You were chosen for a reason and you'll soon know why."

Haman was the king's prime minister,
He had a plan that was cruel and sinister.
Haman cast *purim* so he could choose
The date he'd murder all the Jews.

When Mordecai learned of Haman's plan,
He said to his niece, "You must understand,
You're the only hope to save us all,
Approach the king, do not wait for his call."

Esther took Ahashuerus aside
And said, "My king, you made me your bride.
And now, my king, if your love is true,
You must stop Haman, 'cause I'm also a Jew."

The Jews prevailed and Haman was hanged,
And this is the victory song they sang:
"Grogger, grogger, make a great noise,
Haman is gone, and we Jews rejoice!"

# Twelve Verses

I want to see
How smart you are.
How many strings on
A twelve-string guitar?

There were twelve tribes in Israel
When we entered the Land.
How some disappeared
We still don't understand.

Moses sent out
Twelve Hebrew spies,
But only Caleb and Joshua
Turned out to be wise.

On Halloween,
When the clock strikes twelve,
The world is filled
With ghosts and elves.

King David had a harp
That had twelve strings.
He played and he sang
Of many things.

Look at a calendar,
And one thing becomes clear.
You need twelve months
Or it isn't a whole year.

A baker's dozen
Is kind of obscene
Because you ask for twelve
But you get thirteen.

If next to your hand
You carefully put
Twelve inchworms,
Would you then have a foot?

When the clock strikes twelve,
Is it morning or night?
If you want to get to school,
You had better be right.

If I gave you
A size twelve shoe,
You could make do with one
Instead of two.

A cake with twelve candles—
Your birthday is here!
We send love and good wishes
Throughout the year.

There's a big fat dictionary
There on the shelf.
If you want more verses
You'll have to write them yourself.

# Letters from the Minnesota Tooth Fairy

Dear Allison,

    I heard from my friend the Boulder Tooth Fairy that you lost a tooth. Here's a song you can sing when you lose a tooth. I just made it up. I'll bet you know the tune.

Lost my tooth, what'll I do?
Lost my tooth, what'll I do?
Lost my tooth, what'll I do?
Skip to the dentist, my darling.

Put it under your pillow, and try not to chew,
Put it under your pillow, and try not to chew,
Put it under your pillow, and try not to chew,
Skip to the dentist, my darling.

And during the night, I'll visit you,
And during the night, I'll visit you,
And during the night, I'll visit you,
Skip to the dentist, my darling.

I'll take the tooth and leave money for you,
I'll take the tooth and leave money for you,
I'll take the tooth and leave money for you,
Skip to the dentist, my darling.

Love,

The Minneapolis Tooth Fairy

Dear Allison,

I've had a pretty bad cold for the last two weeks. I've been taking baby-baby-baby aspirin, and my fever has gone down, but it has been very boring for me. I'm looking forward to getting back to work next week. Maybe on Monday.

I read in the *Tooth Fairy Gazette* that it will soon be your birthday. I don't usually do much about birthdays because I'm so busy with teeth, but I've been stuck in the house, with nothing to do, so I thought I'd write you a note and wish you a very happy birthday.

My birthday is in July, but I'm not sure how old I will be. I think it's between two and three hundred years old. I've never had a birthday party myself. Everybody around here is too busy. I may have one when I turn five hundred years old. That's a pretty special birthday, don't you think?

One of these days you will have all of your permanent teeth and you won't be getting any visits from tooth fairies. But don't forget us. I remember your mom and dad from when they were little. I was their tooth fairy, too, when they lived in Minnesota. I wasn't your Bapa's or Mae Mae's tooth fairy. They lived in New York and I never got that far. It wasn't part of my territory.

Well, it has been nice to write to you. I think I feel better already. Happy birthday, and don't forget to brush your teeth. I hate it when I have to collect teeth that haven't been brushed.

Love,

The Minneapolis Tooth Fairy

Dear Allison,

I haven't been able to work all this last week. The reason is a little embarrassing. I lost all of my teeth. Instead of being the tooth fairy, everyone here is calling me the toothless fairy. I really should have been more careful, but I was excited because I saw a very beautiful and unfamiliar bird outside my window, and I wanted to have a better look. So I opened the window and I leaned out, and I leaned, and I leaned, and soon I was on the ground, with my teeth scattered all around me. That was last week. I haven't been able to chew anything and it has been discouraging to watch all the other tooth fairies eating sandwiches and corn on the cob. I love corn on the cob. They eat it in front of me, I think to tease me.

For awhile I had a weird idea. I thought I would make some false teeth out of all of the teeth I had collected from under children's pillows. But the boss tooth fairy told me that would not be sanitary. I tried it anyway, but I looked weird with so many different teeth in my mouth, so I gave up and now I'm just trying to be patient.

Anyway, since I can't work, I thought I would just write you a letter. I know that it is your birthday and so I wish you a happy birthday. If I had any money, I would send you a present, but tooth fairies don't keep money—we just give it away. I was going to send you a tooth necklace, but the boss tooth fairy said that wouldn't be sanitary either. He never lets me do what I want. When I get my teeth back, I might bite him (just kidding!).

Love,

The Minneapolis Tooth Fairy

Dear Allison,

Surprise! I bet you never expected to hear from me again—at least not until you have children of your own. It has been a long, long time since I last wrote to you. I am probably breaking the rules by doing so. You certainly don't have any spare teeth to put under your pillow for me to collect. At least I hope you don't! But—and I'm blushing as I write this—I miss you. Whenever we learned that you had lost a tooth, I always pleaded with the boss fairy to be the one to visit you. You were always so excited and appreciative of what I left, not like some greedy kids who could never be satisfied. And you had such a lovely, expectant smile when you looked under your pillow. I don't mind admitting that I fell a little in love with you. There, I've said it.

I have kept up on your doings in the *Tooth Fairy Gazette*, the newspaper we get up here— newspaper, not one of those blogs or electronic things. I'm old-fashioned, but that's how I prefer to get my news. And I love the ink stains on my hands. They make the news seem more real. Anyway, you outgrew me, but I never outgrew you. I've kept up. I know about your wonderful mom, how she died so young, when you were still a child, only ten years old and Zach was eight. I think I once wrote you that I was your mom's tooth fairy too, when she was growing up in Minneapolis. I loved her too. She was so kind and generous. I felt awful when I learned she had died. I would have written you a letter, but Boss said I wasn't allowed. I wish I had anyway.

These days I'm not so worried about the rules, and I have a lot of free time to reminisce and think about things. I've retired from the tooth fairy business. That's a nice way to put it. Actually, I was fired: Too old, too slow, too forgetful, too mischievous. I know that eventually everyone has to retire, but I had hundreds of years left on my contract.

To tell you the truth, I've been depressed. With all this time on my hands, I don't know what to do with myself. I've been thinking of writing a memoir. I've had lots of interesting experiences in all my years on the job. A memoir would be a good thing to write. Everybody and his uncle are writing memoirs these days. I'm having trouble getting started, however. Hence, this letter (I'm so glad to have the chance to use "hence" in a sentence). I'm warming up by writing to you.

I won't pretend I was blameless. After so many years on the job, the same thing every night: find a tooth, retrieve the tooth, leave some money under the pillow. Never get to say hello to the person you're doing the transaction for. Never shake hands, give or receive a hug. Just do the business and slink away quietly. It got to me. I started doing things that were definitely not in the *Tooth Fairy Handbook*. I wanted to add a little spice to my life—for all of us tooth fairies. Was that so awful?

One time, on my way back from a tooth-to-money transaction, I spotted a whole set of false teeth in a glass next to the bedside of an elderly woman. What the heck, I thought. I'm going to have some fun. So I grabbed the teeth and left a ten-dollar bill and a tooth fairy calling card under her pillow. Imagine her look when she awoke the next morning and started looking for her teeth. I thought it was hilarious. Boss, it turned out, didn't have much of a sense of humor and I was sent to return those teeth pronto. And the ten dollars came out of my pay check. For awhile I was banished from Minnesota and sent out to some countries whose names I can't even pronounce. I couldn't keep track of the currency—I handed out rupees when it should have been pesos or maybe kroner or ringgsit. I was assigned to very poor sections and some of the teeth were just awful to handle. I don't blame the people, they couldn't help themselves, but still....Ugh.

I finally got back to Minnesota, but by then I was a little addled. The first day back on the job in Minnesota, I still had a pocket full of rupees and the kids were crestfallen when they looked under their pillow the next morning—except for one kid who had just come from India because his dad was studying at the University of Minnesota. His family was delighted, but that didn't cut any slack with Boss. By then nothing I did was right.

I got into my worst trouble when I wasn't even on the job. I'm embarrassed to write about it, but I can't keep anything from you. Somehow I know you'll understand. You remember the fairy who supposedly lived in that tiny tree trunk around Lake Harriet? There was a door cut into the tree and kids used to leave little notes for the fairy, and then a day or so later my cousin (did you know she was my cousin?), she would leave a return note. Well, she didn't really live in that tree. That was fake. She lived in a luxury condo up here, not far from me. But she was considered special and she had a chauffeur and a private helicopter that she could use to get back and forth from Lake Harriet. She had a whole staff of apprentice fairies who wrote most of the letters, though she got all the credit—written up in the newspaper, even.

I couldn't see what made her so much better, more special, than the rest of us working fairies, and, to tell the truth, I was jealous. There, I said it. Not only did she get all this attention and affection, she actually got letters from grateful kids or their parents. But who ever wrote to me? No one, that's who. Us tooth fairies (or should it be "we" tooth fairies? I'll have to get that right when I write my memoir), we toiled in the dark and never got a thank-you note; we didn't get any glory or appreciation. We were supposed to do our job and be quiet about it. Well, I guess that's fine, but I did want to get a little recognition for all my efforts, an occasional acknowledgment that I too was doing important work.

One day I just got fed up with how great the tree fairy was, and how much the children loved her, and how selfless and generous she was, and all that. That night, after work, I snuck down to that tree and pulled the door off its hinges and flung it into the lake. The next day the newspaper reported that a mighty wind had blown the door off and a kind person replaced it. OK, I thought, I can play that game. I can be a "mighty wind," and the next night I attacked that door again. This time the news reports were considering vandalism. I think *justice* would have been a better word. Anyway, once again someone replaced the door, and that just made me more mad and more determined. This time I didn't even wait until nightfall. Of course by now the fairy police were on the job, and I got caught in the act. That was the end of my career. I was disciplined. Had my wings clipped. And I was shipped off to this retirement home, long before my time.

It's sad. For years—centuries, actually—I faithfully executed my duties, never stinting, always responsible. But no one remembers that. All those years of service, it's as if they didn't exist. Most of my former colleagues shun me now. It wouldn't do their careers any good to associate with me. So I'm all alone, with my memories. And when I call those up, Allison, you are one of the memories that makes me smile, gives me comfort. I wish you were young again and I was still your own, personal Minnesota Tooth Fairy.

Well, that's not going to happen. Maybe, however, when you have children of your own, I can be reinstated. Maybe you could even put in a good word for me. What a joy that would be. For now, all I can do is hope—and think about my memoir. When I get it done, you'll be the first person to get a copy—under your pillow, of course.

Your devoted friend,

The Minnesota Tooth Fairy, Emeritus